the coastal table

the coastal table

RECIPES INSPIRED BY THE FARMLANDS
AND SEASIDE OF SOUTHERN NEW ENGLAND

Karen J. Covey

photographs by Cassandra Birocco

UNION
PARK
PRESS

BOSTON

Union Park Press
Wellesley, MA 02481
www.unionparkpress.com

Printed in China
First Edition

Unless otherwise noted, photography © Cassandra Birocco
Photograph on back cover, opposite page and page 144 © Union Park Press
Photographs on pages vi-x, 2, 6-7, 10, 14, 18, 28-29, 37, 39, 40, 49, 56, 58, 60, 62, 76-77, 93, 96,
101, 102, 106, 108, 110, 112, 120, 122-123, 138, 146, 185, 189, 191, 200, 208, 211, 212-213, 216-217,
218, 222 © Karen J. Covey
Photograph on pages 44, 48, 72-73, 97, 114-115, 124-125, 130-131, 201 © BaLL LunLa/Shutterstock.com
Photographs on pages 69, 116, 118, 197 © Shelby Larsson
Photograph on page 82 © Luis Molinero/Shutterstock.com
Photograph on page 162 © Ian Vecchiotti

Library of Congress Cataloging-in-Publication Data available upon request.
ISBN: 978-1-934598-10-8

Book and cover design by Karen J. Covey

Although the author and Union Park Press have taken all reasonable care in preparing this book,
we make no warranty about the accuracy and completeness of its content and, to the maximum
extent permitted, disclaim all liability arising from its use.

All information in this book was accurate at the time of publication but is subject to change.

Union Park Press titles are also available in a variety of digital formats.
Please visit our website to learn more: www.unionparkpress.com.

for mom + dad

I miss you both every day but know that every time I'm in the kitchen,

a little part of each of you is with me.

with gratitude

One of the best things about writing this cookbook

was that I was able to turn my passion for food into a dream project. Writing this book led me to some amazing farms, artisans, chefs, and winemakers, to all of whom I am eternally grateful.

To those profiled in this book, thank you for allowing me to share your stories. There are countless others that deserve to be included here as well— I only wish I could fit them all in this book.

A special thank you to all of the talented chefs who contributed recipes to this cookbook. I am honored to include each of you. You are inspirational. To Madeline Block, Daniel Hostettler, Ariel Sasso, Sarah Hearn, Lisa Spieldel, Lauren Murphy, and Brendan Roane for your help in gathering the recipes.

A heartfelt thank you to my amazing team at Union Park Press. Nicole Vecchiotti, for being a great publisher, full of patience and vision. Shelby Larsson, for believing in this project and helping to bring it to light. Caitlin Cullerot, Jen Zimmerman, and Deepa Chungi for all your support along the way. My deepest thanks to each of you for your help in crafting my vision into this beautiful book.

To Cass. You made working on this book a dream. Thank you for being a part of it and for making each photograph more enticing than the next.

To all of my testers, your thoughtful feedback and comments made each recipe better: Andrea Pyenson; Karen Mastovsky; Brian Knowles; Scott Raymond; Marcella Nelson; Susan Pizzolato; Georgia Sparling; the Altman-Shortridge family; the Weglowski family; the Bailey family; Sue Cronin; and Dave Hutchings. Thank you for your friendship and for being a part of this with me.

To Amy McCoy, Cathy Walthers, and David Dadekian. Thank you for your friendship and constant support and all the laughs along the way. To Tara Mataraza Desmond, for your invaluable guidance, support, and friendship.

To Michael, the best brother a girl could ask for: I love you very much. To Sandy, for all your love and support.

And to Dave, for your love and support, and your willingness to taste whatever I put in front of you. Thank you for sharing this journey with me, and for your unwavering patience with me through it. I'm grateful to have you by my side each and every day.

table of contents

In my search for a seaside cottage many years ago, I discovered the South Coast of Massachusetts,

the charming stretch of coastline quietly nestled between the border of Rhode Island and the Bourne Bridge leading to Cape Cod.

I'm not sure if it was the quaint, antique homes in the heart of the village or the breathtaking view from Ned's Point Lighthouse, but I fell in love with Mattapoisett immediately. I knew this was a place to call home.

It began as a simple weekend getaway, but it wasn't long before the coast completely took hold of me. I now live here year round, and although the region may be lesser known than its more popular neighbors, it has just as much to offer.

For someone who is passionate about food, there may not be a more exciting place to live than this stretch of the Southern New England coast. In many ways, food is at its center. Dating back to the days of whaling ships and fishing ports, the region is steeped in history. These ships brought immigrants to local shores, most notably the Portuguese, who are now deeply woven into the fabric of this region. Their influences can be found everywhere, especially in Fall River and New Bedford, adding their own flavorful spin to traditional New England dishes.

The New Bedford Seaport is still considered one of the top fishing ports in the United States, and while the South Coast can certainly boast about its amazing seafood, that is only part of the culinary story here. The warm waters of Narragansett and Buzzards bays help control the climate while the mild ocean breeze allows for the longest growing season in all of New England. Countless farmers make their homes here and spend long hours in the fields cultivating and growing some of the best produce found anywhere. Stop by and talk to any one of them at a local farmers' market and you'll see the passion and pride for what they do. Many of these people have lived here for generations, building a future and making a strong commitment to sustainability. The result is that farm stands are so plentiful that it's possible to cook and eat according to the season nearly all year round.

This cookbook will take you on a culinary journey along this remarkable coastline, bringing you to some of the area's best markets, restaurants, and hidden gems. Tour the beautiful wineries, discover

cheesemakers and bakeries, enjoy a simple but delicious meal of fresh seafood while watching the sunset. Most importantly, meet the hardworking, knowledgeable people that are growing, creating, and celebrating the region's offerings. Their enthusiasm and commitment provides inspiration to me in my kitchen each and every day.

I wrote *The Coastal Table* with the hope of encouraging you to venture out and discover these places—and others—on your own. It's a small collection of what the region has to offer, but my hope is that you'll unearth something new along the way—whether it's the incredible beef from Blackbird Farm, the distinctive Cloumage from Shy Brothers Farm, or the unique wines from Travessia Urban Winery in downtown New Bedford.

The recipes in this book reflect the way we eat and live here. Recipes inspired by the ocean, like seared scallops with corn risotto + basil oil, mussels with white wine, butter + sourdough, and baked fish with nasturtium butter, are as perfect for entertaining as they are for weeknight dinners. Summer months are ideal for packing a picnic and heading to the beach; and the abundance of fresh, local produce provides inspiration for portable recipes like quinoa tabbouleh with garden cucumbers, chilled paella salad with shrimp, and a Portuguese-inspired salad of poached tuna, chickpeas + chopped hard-boiled egg. As summer winds down and the air grows cool, big, warm bowls of roasted butternut squash soup with maple cream and slices of afternoon apple-sauce cake with spiced whipped cream will help you usher in fall in the most delicious ways possible.

In addition to my own recipes, some of New England's finest chefs were kind enough to contribute to this book, including Barbara Lynch of the Barbara Lynch Gruppo in Boston; Champe Spiedel of Persimmon in Bristol, RI; and Matthew Jennings of Farmstead/La Laiterie in Providence. These chefs, among others, celebrate the bounty of this region in their cuisine each and every day. I hope this cookbook will inspire you to do the same.

brunch

spicy bloody mary

sunday morning mimosa

deep-dish quiche with onion, spinach + salty feta

baked eggs with fresh thyme, tomatoes + parmesan

cinnamon crumb coffee cake

fresh-picked blueberry muffins

chunky homemade granola

garlic chive scrambled eggs

old-fashioned pancakes with apple butter

sweet bread french toast with honey butter

whole wheat pumpkin scones

bacon jam

black pepper biscuits

One of the greatest benefits

of living along New England's coast is that you can always count on having a house full of guests. Visitors will arrive for summer weekends, fall excursions, and restful winter breaks spent by a fire. This chapter represents some of my favorite brunch recipes, perfect for kicking off a relaxing weekend with friends and family, no matter the season.

spicy bloody mary

SERVES 6

The quintessential start to any brunch is always a good Bloody Mary, and I prefer mine with a little kick. Ideally, a Bloody Mary should have a rich, deep flavor, but not so much spice that it overwhelms the other ingredients. It's the perfect cocktail to make for weekend entertaining because you can make a big batch ahead of time—in fact, the longer the flavors develop, the better it will be.

8 celery stalks (2 with leaves), divided
2 lemons
2 tablespoons plus 2 teaspoons horseradish
2 tablespoons plus 2 teaspoons Tabasco, or to taste
1 tablespoon Worcestershire sauce
1 tablespoon finely minced onion
   Kosher salt, to taste
   Freshly ground black pepper, to taste
2 cups vodka, or to taste
46 ounces tomato juice

1. Trim 6 celery stalks so that they fit standing up in 6 tall serving glasses. Place one stalk in each glass.
2. Cut 1 lemon into 6 thin slices. Place 1 lemon slice into each serving glass and place glasses in refrigerator to chill.
3. Roughly dice remaining 2 celery stalks and leaves. Place in bowl of a food processor and purée until finely minced (this can also be done by hand). Transfer to a large serving pitcher and add juice of remaining lemon, horseradish, Tabasco, Worcestershire sauce, and onion. Stir and season with salt and pepper. Add tomato juice and stir to incorporate. Chill for at least 1 hour to allow flavors to develop.
4. Taste and adjust for seasonings and spice level before serving. Add ice to each serving glass. Divide vodka among glasses and fill each with Bloody Mary mixture. Serve cold.

cook's note: You can also stir in the vodka before you chill the pitcher, but adding the alcohol to each glass gives you the option of serving it "virgin" to anyone who may want it that way.

sunday morning mimosa

SERVES 4

Life on the coast is relaxed—Sunday mornings especially. Deep mugs of freshly brewed coffee and the Sunday paper usually start the day, and on special occasions, mimosas follow. I prefer mimosas in the cooler months, while I'm in the kitchen making a hearty brunch and easing into a day of watching football. These brightly colored cocktails made with blood oranges—a fruit I fell in love with during a trip to Sicily—are vibrant enough to bring a little warmth to an otherwise chilly morning. During blood orange season (usually December to March), the tart and slight berry-like flavor of this fruit is a nice alternative to fresh orange juice.

1/4 cup freshly squeezed blood orange juice (from approximately 1-2 medium blood oranges)
1   bottle Westport Brut (or a champagne or other sparkling wine), chilled

1. Place 4 champagne flutes (or desired serving glasses) in refrigerator and chill for at least 30 minutes.
2. Carefully add 1 tablespoon of blood orange juice to bottom of each glass. Top with champagne and serve immediately.

cook's note: Blood oranges last longer when stored in the refrigerator.

westport rivers vineyard, westport, ma

The first thing visitors are struck by when approaching Westport Rivers Vineyard is the utter beauty of the surroundings; the beautiful antique homes and rolling, patchwork fields bordering Hixbridge Road seem to guide you to the vineyard. And while the scenery is stunning, chances are it is the wine that has brought you here. Owned and operated by the Russell Family for four generations, Westport Rivers sets the standard for winemaking in New England.

Intentionally situated on a breathtaking plot of south-facing land that hugs the coastline, the vineyard takes full advantage of its geography. The soil is dark, rich New England loam on well-drained gravel, and the warm waters of the Gulf Stream help to control the climate. Those gentle ocean breezes and moderate temperatures provide for a longer growing season, which is perfect for the vineyard's award-winning wines. The vineyard is best known for its sparkling wines, especially the Westport Brut RJR, which has been served multiple times at the White House, and its outstanding Chardonnay.

This region of Southern New England is often compared to the Alsace or Loire Valley regions of France. In fact, this pocket of New England is perfectly suited for similar crisp, aromatic white wines. (Big, bold reds don't stand a chance here.) The vineyard keeps most of the grapes for its own wines, bottling up to seven thousand cases annually, but sells off the rest of what they don't need to other area winemakers.

The vineyard is open for tours and tastings, and during the summer it's the perfect place to bring a picnic. The grounds are a beautiful spot for lounging with friends and family, sipping a glass of wine, and enjoying the pristine views of the vineyard. Tastings are held year round, both outside and inside the picturesque 19th century farmhouse, where you can buy bottles to take home and browse through the art gallery featuring works of local artists.

deep-dish quiche with onion, spinach + salty feta

SERVES 4-6

When I have a house full of guests, I love to wake up early to make this for brunch. Although this quiche takes some time to prepare, it's well worth the effort (and you can always make the dough the day before to give yourself a head start). The unexpected height of this deep-dish version makes for a beautiful centerpiece on your breakfast table. For this recipe, I prefer to use a local feta brined in sea salt from Narragansett Creamery in Rhode Island. Of course, any salty feta will work.

Dough
2 cups flour, plus extra for dusting
1/4 teaspoon sugar
1/4 teaspoon kosher salt
1½ sticks unsalted butter, chilled and cut into small pieces
1 extra large egg, white and yolk separated
1/4 cup plus 2 tablespoons ice water, or more if necessary

Filling
2 tablespoons extra virgin olive oil
1 medium onion, thinly sliced
Kosher salt, to taste
Freshly ground black pepper, to taste
3 cups packed fresh baby spinach
8 extra large eggs
1½ cups milk
1½ cups heavy cream
4 ounces crumbled feta cheese

1. Make dough. In a food processor, combine flour, sugar, and salt. Add butter and pulse until mixture becomes coarse crumbs, about 10 seconds. Add egg yolk (reserve egg white) and mix again. With machine running, add 1/4 cup ice water, one tablespoon at a time, in a slow, steady stream through feed tube. Pulse until dough holds together, no more than 30 seconds. Dough should not be wet or sticky. Test finished dough by squeezing a small amount together to see if it holds its shape. If still crumbly, add more ice water, 1 tablespoon at a time.
2. Wrap dough in plastic wrap and flatten slightly into a disc. Refrigerate for about 1 hour, or overnight if making dough ahead of time.
3. On a lightly floured surface, gently roll dough into a 15-inch circle, about 1/4-inch thick. Carefully fold dough in half over rolling pin and use it to transfer dough to a 9-inch springform pan with 3-inch sides. Place dough so it is evenly centered over pan and gently drapes into pan. Using your fingers, press dough firmly against bottom and up sides of pan, covering completely, taking care not to make any holes in dough. Press dough together wherever necessary to form a nice, uniform edge all around top of pan (trim off any excess or uneven pieces). Place pan on a baking sheet and set aside.
4. Preheat oven to 400°F.
5. Make filling. In a large sauté pan, heat olive oil over medium heat. Add onion and cook until softened, about 7-10 minutes, and season with salt and pepper. Add spinach and cook until just wilted, about 2-3 minutes. Remove from heat and allow to cool slightly.
6. In a large bowl, add eggs and reserved egg white. Beat by hand (or with a mixer) until frothy. Stir in milk and cream and season with a pinch of salt and pepper. Beat again until light and frothy, about 3-4 minutes.
7. Scatter feta cheese evenly over bottom of crust, followed by cooled onion and spinach mixture. Carefully pour egg mixture over top. Cover with aluminum foil and bake for 1 hour. Remove foil, rotate pan, and continue to bake until quiche has set but still has a slight jiggle in center and is golden brown around edges, about 25-30 minutes. (Check after 15 minutes and cover again with aluminum foil if top is getting too brown.)
8. Remove from oven and allow to cool for 10-15 minutes before serving. If making quiche in advance, allow to cool to room temperature, then remove it from pan until ready to serve.

cook's note: Quiche is a great canvas for anything you find fresh at the market or for what you already have in the refrigerator. Almost anything will work, so feel free to be creative.

baked eggs with fresh thyme, tomatoes + parmesan

SERVES 4

I have a weakness for oozing, runny egg yolks, and this simple breakfast dish has become one of my favorites, especially when I have a fresh baguette to soak up all the deliciousness at the bottom of my dish. While the bursts of color from the tomatoes make this a beautiful dish for a late summer morning, this recipe is extremely versatile. You can substitute the basic components with just about anything: try other fresh herbs, such as chives or parsley; different cheeses, like goat cheese or freshly grated sharp cheddar; cooked and finely diced ham or bacon; or even some sautéed vegetables. Almost anything goes—and if you're cooking for a crowd, you can customize each dish according to preference.

8   extra large eggs
2   tablespoons unsalted butter
4   tablespoons heavy cream
2   teaspoons minced fresh thyme
12 small cherry tomatoes, cut in half
4   tablespoons freshly grated Parmesan
    Kosher salt, to taste
    Freshly ground black pepper, to taste
8   1-inch thick slices toasted French bread, for serving

1. Preheat broiler to high and place an oven rack on top shelf (about 6 inches from top).
2. Gather 4 small bowls and carefully crack 2 eggs into each bowl, keeping yolks intact. (You won't be cooking in these dishes but you'll want eggs cracked and ready to go before you start.)
3. Place 4 shallow, oven-safe gratin dishes on a baking pan. Place ½ tablespoon of butter and 1 tablespoon of cream in each dish.
4. Place baking pan under broiler until butter has melted and mixture is warm and bubbly, about 1-2 minutes. Carefully remove pan from oven and gently transfer 2 eggs into each gratin dish, taking care not to break yolks. Sprinkle each with equal amounts of thyme, tomatoes, and Parmesan and season with salt and pepper.
5. Place pan back under broiler and cook until whites of eggs are almost set, about 5 minutes (check after 2-3 minutes and cover with aluminum foil if tops are getting too brown).
6. Remove from oven and allow to cool for about 30 seconds (eggs will continue to cook after you remove them from oven). Carefully transfer each dish to a serving plate and serve warm with toasted bread for dipping.

cook's note: While you can find a good baguette just about anywhere, Pain d'Avignon makes my favorite. Founded in 1992, Pain D'Avignon uses Old World traditions to craft a variety of breads that truly complement every meal. You can stop by the Hyannis bakery to buy them (and definitely grab a croissant or two while you're there!), but they are also a regular at farmers' markets throughout the region—including markets in Boston and all over the Cape—as well as at quality vendors, such as Lee's Market in Westport, MA.

cinnamon crumb coffee cake

SERVES 8

No matter the season or the crowd, this cake is a welcome addition to any breakfast table. Its soft, buttery texture, layered with sugary bursts of cinnamon crumb streusel, is perfect for company—or left on the counter for that enticing afternoon slice. As with most baked goods, it's best enjoyed the day it's made or shortly thereafter.

1½ sticks plus 1 tablespoon unsalted butter, divided, at room temperature
2½ cups flour, plus extra for dusting
1 tablespoon baking powder
1 teaspoon baking soda
½ teaspoon kosher salt
1½ cups sugar
3 extra large eggs, at room temperature
1 teaspoon vanilla extract
1¼ cups sour cream

Streusel
1 cup packed light brown sugar
¾ cup flour
1½ teaspoons ground cinnamon
1 teaspoon kosher salt
6 tablespoons cold unsalted butter, diced

1. Preheat oven to 350°F.
2. Grease a 10-inch tube pan (or angel food cake pan) evenly with 1 tablespoon butter. Dust with flour, evenly coating buttered pan. Shake out any excess flour and set aside.
3. In a medium bowl, combine flour, baking powder, baking soda, and salt and set aside.
4. In bowl of a stand mixer fitted with paddle attachment, cream together remaining 1½ sticks butter and sugar until well combined, about 5 minutes. Add eggs, vanilla, and sour cream. Gradually add flour mixture, mixing after each addition. Mix until just combined.
5. Make streusel. In a medium bowl, combine brown sugar, flour, cinnamon, and salt. Using a pastry cutter, fork, or by hand, cut in butter until coarse crumbs form.
6. Spoon half of batter into prepared pan, carefully spreading it into an even layer. (Batter will be thick so be sure to run your spatula under warm water to help distribute it.) Scatter half of streusel topping evenly over top, followed by remaining half of batter. Carefully spread batter out evenly to cover streusel topping. Top with remaining half of streusel topping.
7. Bake until a toothpick comes out clean, about 45-50 minutes. Remove from oven and allow to cool for 15-20 minutes before removing from pan. Allow to cool completely to room temperature before serving.

fresh-picked blueberry muffins

MAKES 6 LARGE MUFFINS

I started my own tradition of picking fresh blueberries when I moved to the South Coast, and ever since, it's something I look forward to every year. I love being out there, searching through the bushes for the most perfect, plump blueberries and hearing the sound they make as they plunk into the brightly colored bucket hanging from my neck. I always leave with more than I need, but having too many blueberries is never a bad thing. They're a perfect (and super healthy) snack and they freeze well, providing me with a nice reminder of the warm months in which they were picked. But when they're fresh, blueberries call to be added to muffin batter.

Cooking spray
3 cups flour
1 tablespoon baking powder
1/2 teaspoon kosher salt
6 tablespoons unsalted butter, at room temperature
1 1/4 cups sugar
2 large eggs
2 tablespoons vegetable oil
1 1/2 teaspoons vanilla extract
1 cup milk
1 pint (2 cups) fresh blueberries
Turbinado sugar, for garnish, optional

1. Preheat oven to 375°F.
2. Spray a large 6-cup muffin pan with cooking spray and set aside.
3. In a bowl, whisk together flour, baking powder, and salt and set aside.
4. Using an electric mixer fitted with paddle attachment, cream butter and sugar together on medium speed. Add eggs, one at a time, vegetable oil, and vanilla and mix until fluffy, about 1-2 minutes.
5. Reduce speed to low. Add 1/3 flour mixture and mix until completely incorporated. Add 1/2 of milk and mix until completely incorporated. Add another 1/3 flour mixture and mix again, followed by remaining 1/2 of milk, and then remaining 1/3 flour mixture, mixing well after each addition to incorporate. Remove bowl from mixer and gently fold in blueberries.
6. Divide batter among muffin tins and sprinkle tops of each one with turbinado sugar (if using).
7. Bake until muffins are golden brown, 30-35 minutes (check after 20-25 minutes and cover with aluminum foil if tops are getting too brown).
8. Remove from oven and allow to cool in pan for 15 minutes. Remove from pan and transfer to wire rack to cool completely. Once cooled, the muffins are best eaten the same day they are made.

cook's note: You can make this recipe as 12 regular-sized muffins as well. Simply adjust the cooking time to 20-25 minutes.

chunky homemade granola

MAKES APPROXIMATELY 8 CUPS

It seems as though every cook has a granola recipe, and I'm no different. Making homemade granola is surprisingly easy, and you can customize it any way you like. I often make batches of granola using what I have on hand in the kitchen or based on the flavors of the season. This version uses oil, which tends to make a crispier (and chunkier) granola, especially if you don't toss it around it as it cooks. It's great for breakfast but also easy to eat by the handful, which makes it a great snack for beach days and hiking excursions.

	Cooking spray
6	cups old-fashioned oats
1	cup unsalted whole almonds, roughly chopped
1	cup shredded, sweetened coconut
1/4	cup finely ground flaxseed or wheat germ, optional
1	teaspoon kosher salt
3/4	cup packed light brown sugar
3/4	cup honey
1/4	cup plus 2 tablespoons vegetable or canola oil
1	tablespoon vanilla extract

1. Preheat oven to 300°F.
2. Line a baking sheet with parchment paper, coat top of paper with cooking spray, and set aside.
3. In a large bowl, combine oats, almonds, coconut, flaxseed or wheat germ (if using), and salt.
4. In a medium bowl, combine sugar, honey, oil, and vanilla and stir until combined. Pour over oat mixture and mix until evenly coated. Pour granola onto baking sheet and, using a spatula, press granola firmly. Bake, without stirring, until outside edges are just golden brown, about 30-35 minutes. (Start checking after 25 minutes to avoid overcooking.)
5. Remove from oven and allow granola to cool completely before breaking it apart into chunks. Granola can be stored in an airtight container for up to 2 weeks.

cook's note: Ground flaxseed or wheat germ are a quick (and easy) way to incorporate additional nutrients.

garlic chive scrambled eggs

SERVES 4

I prefer to make my scrambled eggs with cream (or half and half) because it provides a rich, smooth texture. The addition of fresh herbs brightens up the dish, and just about anything growing in your container garden works: thyme, parsley, or chives. But in the summer months, when garlic chives are in season, I like to use these overlooked herbs. Garlic chives have a mellow, garlic taste and are flatter (and not hollow) like traditional chives. They add a delicious, subtle flavor to simple scrambled eggs.

8	extra large eggs
2	tablespoons cream (or half and half)
	Kosher salt, to taste
	Freshly ground black pepper, to taste
2	tablespoons unsalted butter
1	tablespoon diced garlic chives
	Multigrain toast, for serving, optional

1. In a large bowl, crack eggs. Add cream and, using a fork, gently whisk until thoroughly combined and eggs are pale yellow in color. Do not over mix. Season with salt and pepper.
2. Add butter to a medium non-stick pan and place over medium-high heat. When foaming starts to subside, gently swirl butter around pan, coating as much of bottom as possible. Add eggs and allow them to cook for about 10-15 seconds without disturbing.
3. Using a heat-proof spatula or a wooden spoon, begin scraping eggs from edges and stir continuously until eggs are almost set. Stir in garlic chives and continue cooking until eggs are creamy and soft (or until desired consistency).
4. Remove pan from heat, divide eggs among serving plates, season with a pinch of additional salt and pepper, and serve warm.

old-fashioned pancakes with apple butter

MAKES 4 LARGE PANCAKES

Big, fluffy pancakes are just the beginning of a great breakfast; what you put on top of them is equally important. This apple butter is a nice alternative to the old standbys of butter and maple syrup, especially in the fall when you have a basket of freshly picked apples on hand. While traditional apple butter is made by stewing the apples slowly for hours until they are concentrated and dark brown, this quicker version is more like a compound butter, which is a perfect way to capture all those sweet autumn flavors in much less time. I prefer to use a McIntosh apple for this recipe, but any sweet variety of apple works as well. Make the butter a bit in advance; it will keep for up to 3 days in the refrigerator.

Apple Butter

1   stick plus 1 tablespoon unsalted butter, divided, at room temperature
1   medium McIntosh apple, peeled, cored, and cut into $1/2$-inch cubes
1   tablespoon light brown sugar
2   tablespoons water, divided
1   teaspoon ground cinnamon
$1/2$ teaspoon ground nutmeg
     Pinch of ground cloves
     Pinch of kosher salt

3   tablespoons unsalted butter, divided
2   cups flour
1   tablespoon baking powder
1   tablespoon sugar
$1/2$ teaspoon kosher salt
2   cups milk
1   large egg
1   teaspoon vanilla extract

1. Make apple butter. In a medium saucepan, melt 1 tablespoon butter over medium heat. Add apples, brown sugar, and 1 tablespoon water and cook until softened, about 12 minutes. Stir apples every so often to make sure they don't stick to pan. You should be able to easily pierce apples with a fork when done. If you cannot, cook for another 1-2 minutes. Add cinnamon, nutmeg, cloves, and salt and toss together with apples, coating completely. Add remaining 1 tablespoon water, stir to incorporate, and cook for another 30 seconds. Remove from heat and allow to cool, at least 1 hour.
2. Transfer apple mixture to a food processor along with remaining 1 stick softened butter and process until almost smooth (it should be a little chunky). Transfer butter to a serving bowl, cover with plastic wrap, and refrigerate, at least 1 hour. Bring to room temperature before serving.
3. Make pancakes. In a small saucepan, melt 2 tablespoons butter. Set aside to cool.
4. Preheat oven to 200°F. Place a baking sheet in oven (to keep cooked pancakes warm).
5. Preheat a griddle or large non-stick pan over medium heat.
6. In a medium bowl, combine flour, baking powder, sugar, and salt and set aside.
7. In another medium bowl, combine $1 3/4$ cups milk, egg, vanilla, and melted butter. Slowly add egg mixture to flour mixture and mix until just combined (batter will be thick, so stir in another few tablespoons of milk if you prefer a thinner consistency).
8. Melt remaining 1 tablespoon butter in pan. Spoon batter into any size pancakes you like and cook until bottoms are just browned (and bubbles start to appear around edges of pancakes), about 3-4 minutes. Using a spatula, flip pancakes and cook until second side is lightly browned. Transfer pancakes to warm baking sheet in oven. Repeat with remaining batter.
9. Top with apple butter and serve warm.

JONNY CAKES: A RHODE ISLAND STAPLE

Jonny cakes (sometimes spelled "johnnycakes") are unleavened cornmeal pancakes made from cornmeal and water (sometimes milk, sugar, or salt are added as well), griddled, and served with butter and syrup. They are so popular in Rhode Island that it is hard to find a breakfast menu where they are not featured.

Many believe that Jonny cakes are so named because of their ability to travel along with early settlers and were once called "journey cakes." Another theory is that the name stems from "joniken," an American Indian word for corn. Regardless, they have become a staple throughout the region. There are several brands of Jonny cake meal available, but Gray's Grist Mill and Kenyon's Grist Mill are likely the oldest and best known in the country.

Dating back to 1746, Gray's Grist Mill has been located in Adamsville, RI…sort of. Believe it or not, the state line separating Rhode Island from Massachusetts runs directly through the mill pond, so both states claim it as a historical treasure.

What may be more interesting about Gray's Grist Mill, however, is that its cornmeal is made from Rhode Island Narragansett Flint Corn. Flint corn is grown on the southern coast of Rhode Island, where soft breezes impart the grains with their renowned flavor. Originally a species of wild grass domesticated by American Indians, white cap flint corn is notoriously difficult to grow and a challenge to grind because of its rock-hard kernels.

One reason why this corn is so finicky is that it can't be grown near any other variety of corn. It's a pure breed of corn, which reproduces by open-air pollination and mutates on contact with any other strains. It generally produces very low yields, as well.

Purists will decry any Jonny cake meal that fails to use Rhode Island-grown flint corn, but many Rhode Islanders are partial to Kenyon's Grist Mill brand, despite the fact that the corn is from Virginia.

Nestled along the banks of the Queen's River in the village of Usquepaugh, RI, Kenyon's Grist Mill makes its cornmeal the old-fashioned way on the original granite millstones quarried from Westerly, RI. The granite helps produce an exceptional texture and quality not found in steel-ground flours. Kenyon's uses a single-pass stone grinding process that preserves the vital, natural nutrition of the grains.

No matter which brand you prefer, these little cakes are rooted deep in the area's history and have established a rightful place on Rhode Island's breakfast counter.

sweet bread french toast with honey butter

SERVES 4

During the early 19th century, Portuguese settlers came to the east coast of Southern New England, where they became a vital part of the fishing and whaling communities. Their influence is still an important part of the culture in this region, particularly when it comes to culinary traditions. Portuguese sweet bread is a pale yellow, cake-like bread that is most often made with a bit of honey and/or vanilla. The flavors of this French toast recipe mimic the flavors of the bread itself. Lemon zest in the soaking liquid adds a bright, unexpected note that complements the sweetness of the bread, and the honey butter is a flavorful alternative to maple syrup. The butter will keep in the refrigerator for up to 3 days.

Honey Butter
4	tablespoons (1/2 stick) unsalted butter, at room temperature
2	teaspoons honey

2	extra large (or 3 large) eggs
1/2	cup milk
2	teaspoons honey
1	teaspoon vanilla extract
	Zest of 1/2 lemon
	Pinch kosher salt
4	1-inch thick slices sweet bread, from a small loaf (see cook's note)
	1-2 tablespoons unsalted butter

1. Make honey butter. In a medium bowl, combine softened butter with honey and mix until well combined. Transfer to a small serving dish, cover with plastic wrap, and refrigerate until ready to use.
2. In a large casserole dish, combine eggs, milk, honey, vanilla, lemon zest, and salt. Whisk together until well combined. Place bread slices in casserole and allow to soak for no more than 15 seconds per side (see cook's note).
3. Meanwhile, in a large non-stick pan, heat butter over medium heat.
4. Remove honey butter from refrigerator and allow it to come to room temperature.
5. Add bread slices and cook until golden brown, about 5 minutes per side. Transfer French toast to a large serving platter and serve warm with honey butter.

cook's note: Sweet bread is available in large loafs all over Southern New England, and sometimes you can find smaller loaves in certain Portuguese markets. You can make this recipe with either, but I prefer the smaller loaves when I can find them because they often hold up better when making the French toast. Regardless of which you use, it's important to soak the bread for no more than 15 seconds per side or this delicate bread will fall apart. Depending on the size of your pan, soak only the number of slices that will fit at one time. If your pan can hold all 4 slices at the same time, soak all 4 pieces; if it can only hold 2 slices, soak and cook 2, then place in a 200°F oven to stay warm while you soak and cook the remaining 2 slices.

whole wheat pumpkin scones

MAKES 8 SCONES

My father made some of the best scones I've ever had, so it's no surprise that my love of this tempting breakfast treat comes from him. While I like to experiment with different flavors throughout the seasons, this is my favorite when autumn sets in. Using whole wheat pastry flour keeps the scones light and makes them less of a guilty pleasure.

2   cups whole wheat pastry flour
1/2   cup sugar
1   tablespoon baking powder
1/2   teaspoon kosher salt
3/4   teaspoon ground cinnamon, divided
1/2   teaspoon ground nutmeg
1/2   teaspoon ground ginger
1/8   teaspoon ground cloves
6   tablespoons unsalted cold butter, cut into pieces
1/2   cup canned pumpkin
3-4   tablespoons heavy cream, divided
1   extra large egg
1   teaspoon vanilla extract
1-2   teaspoons turbinado sugar, for garnish

1. Preheat oven to 425°F.
2. Line a baking sheet with parchment paper and set aside.
3. In a large bowl, combine flour, sugar, baking powder, salt, 1/2 teaspoon cinnamon, nutmeg, ginger, and cloves. Using a pastry cutter, fork, or by hand, cut in butter and mix until coarse crumbs form. Be sure to do this fairly quickly so butter stays nice and cold.
4. In a medium bowl, whisk together pumpkin, 2 tablespoons heavy cream, egg, and vanilla until well combined.
5. Fold wet ingredients into dry ingredients, then form dough into a ball (dough should hold together nicely and not be too crumbly). Stir in an additional 1 tablespoon of cream if the dough is too dry.
6. Turn dough out onto a lightly floured surface and form into a circle, about 1-inch thick. Cut dough into 8 equal wedges. Place on prepared baking sheet, leaving about 1/2-inch space between them. Brush tops with remaining 1 tablespoon cream.
7. In a small bowl, combine turbinado sugar and remaining 1/4 teaspoon cinnamon. Sprinkle a bit of cinnamon sugar over top of each wedge and bake until golden brown and a toothpick inserted into center comes out clean, about 15-20 minutes. Remove from oven and allow scones to cool slightly before serving.

cook's note: You can make smaller scones by using a cookie cutter and cutting the dough into smaller rounds. Turbinado sugar (or sugar in the raw) gives the scones an unexpected sweet surprise on top.

bacon jam

MAKES APPROXIMATELY 1 CUP

This thick, smoky bacon jam has undertones of coffee and maple, making it a perfect condiment for just about anything. Serve it with black pepper biscuits, on top of a burger, or spread on fresh bread for an over-the-top grilled cheese. It's so good it will become a fixture on your table. The bacon jam will keep for 2 weeks in your refrigerator (but it won't last that long).

8	strips thick-cut Applewood smoked bacon, roughly chopped
1/2	small onion, diced
	Kosher salt, to taste
	Freshly ground black pepper, to taste
2	cloves garlic, minced
1/4	cup apple cider
2	teaspoons balsamic vinegar
1/4	cup brewed coffee, cooled
1/4	cup brown sugar
2	tablespoons maple syrup
2	teaspoons Dijon mustard

1. In a medium saucepan, add bacon and cook over medium heat, stirring as needed, until nicely browned. Remove with a slotted spoon, transfer to a bowl, and set aside.
2. Pour off and discard all but 1 tablespoon of grease from pan.
3. Add onions to remaining bacon grease and cook until softened, about 5 minutes. Season with salt and pepper. Add garlic and cook for another 1-2 minutes. Carefully add apple cider and balsamic vinegar to deglaze pan, scraping browned bits from bottom of pan. Add coffee, brown sugar, maple syrup, and mustard and stir to combine.
4. Add bacon back to pan. Cook over medium heat until mixture has thickened and reaches consistency of a jam, about 10-15 minutes (cook a bit longer if necessary). Set aside to cool to room temperature.

cook's note: For a more spreadable consistency, transfer cooked mixture to a food processor and pulse until smooth or slightly chunky.

black pepper biscuits

MAKES 6 LARGE BISCUITS

Hints of black pepper add a spicy undertone
to these big, flaky biscuits. I like to serve them
warm from the oven for breakfast, as an indulgent
side with sausage and gravy, or with garlic chive
scrambled eggs (see page 19). They also make
an excellent sandwich with ham and a smear
of Dijon mustard. I prefer to cut the biscuits into
squares (especially if planning to use them for
sandwiches) but any shape works.

   Cooking spray
2   cups flour, plus extra for dusting
1   tablespoon plus 1 teaspoon baking powder
1   tablespoon sugar
1   teaspoon freshly ground black pepper,
   plus extra for garnish
1/2 teaspoon baking soda
1/2 teaspoon kosher salt
1   stick cold unsalted butter, cubed
1   cup milk, plus extra for brushing

1. Preheat oven to 425°F.
2. Coat a baking sheet with cooking spray and
   set aside.
3. In a mixing bowl, combine flour, baking powder,
   sugar, pepper, baking soda, and salt.
4. Using a pastry cutter, fork, or by hand, cut in
   butter until coarse crumbs form. Be sure to do this
   fairly quickly, so butter stays cold. (Cold butter
   helps keep biscuits light and flaky.)
5. Make a well in center of flour mixture and pour in
   2/3 cup milk. Gently combine until dough just holds
   together, adding an additional 1 tablespoon milk
   as needed (somewhere between 1-3 tablespoons).
   Do not overwork dough or biscuits will be tough.
6. Turn dough out on lightly floured surface and form
   into a rectangle about 1-inch thick x 5 inches wide
   x 6 inches long. Cut dough into 6 equal squares.
7. Transfer biscuits to prepared baking sheet. Brush
   tops with additional milk and sprinkle each with
   a pinch of black pepper. Bake until golden brown,
   about 10-15 minutes. Serve warm or at room
   temperature.

steamed clams in garlic, lemon + beer broth

soups + sandwiches

new england cioppino with toasted baguette

watch hill oyster chowder

portuguese kale soup

chilled sweet corn soup with lobster

bread + garlic soup with rhubarb compote + garden blossoms

steamed clams in garlic, lemon + beer broth

roasted butternut squash soup with maple cream

garden carrot soup

egg salad tartine with breakfast radishes + chives

serrano + manchego sandwich with quince

tuna niçoise sandwich with crumbled eggs + tomatoes

When such natural beauty surrounds you, there is always some place to explore. I gravitate toward delicious yet simple lunches and dinners in order to get in all the day's activities—whether it's sailing, hiking, a walk on the beach with my dog, or an evening spent around a bonfire. Taking cues from the region's exceptional produce and abundance of fresh seafood, these soups and sandwiches are ideal for casual dinners and relaxed lunches.

new england cioppino with toasted baguette

SERVES 4-6

Cioppino is a hearty fish stew that originates in San Francisco's fishing and immigrant cultures, making it a perfect culinary transport to coastal tables throughout New England. Traditionally, cioppino is made from the catch of the day, meaning that almost any type of fish will work, though it is best when made with a mix of fish that provides variation in both texture and flavor (see cook's note). I like to use puréed tomatoes for the broth, but you can easily substitute with diced tomatoes for even more texture. In this recipe, subtle hints of fennel add unexpected flavor and the toasted baguette is requisite, as you'll need something to sop up the delicious broth at the bottom of the bowl.

4	tablespoons extra virgin olive oil, divided
2	shallots, thinly sliced
1	medium onion, thinly sliced
1	fennel bulb, thinly sliced
	Kosher salt, to taste
	Freshly ground pepper, to taste
2	cloves garlic, finely minced
1/2	cup white wine
1	28-ounce can puréed tomatoes
3-4	cups low-sodium vegetable stock
1	bay leaf
1/2	teaspoon dried fennel seeds
1	tablespoon minced fresh thyme
1	baguette
2	pounds mixed fresh fish (cod, salmon, shrimp, and clams), see cook's note
2	tablespoons minced fresh flat-leaf Italian parsley, for serving
2	tablespoons minced fennel fronds, for serving

1. In a medium saucepan, heat 2 tablespoons olive oil over medium heat. Add shallot, onion, and fennel, and cook until softened, about 5-7 minutes. Season with salt and pepper. Add garlic and cook for another 1-2 minutes. Add wine to deglaze pan, scraping browned bits from bottom of pan.
2. Add tomatoes to pot along with 2 cups of stock, bay leaf, fennel seeds, and thyme, and bring to a boil. Reduce heat to simmer for 10-15 minutes.
3. Preheat oven to 400°F.
4. Cut baguette into four equal pieces. Slice each piece in half, horizontally.
5. Place bread on a large baking sheet and brush top side of each piece with remaining 2 tablespoons olive oil. Cook until golden brown on both sides, about 5-10 minutes. Remove and set aside.
6. Add clams to pot and cook for about 7-10 minutes. When they start to open, add cod and salmon to pot and continue to cook until fish is cooked through, about 5 minutes. Add shrimp and cook for another 2-3 minutes, until shrimp are bright pink and cooked through and clams have fully opened. Add a bit more stock if necessary to make sure fish is covered as it cooks. Discard any unopened clams after cooking.
7. Stir in parsley and fennel fronds and ladle soup into serving bowls. Serve warm with toasted baguette.

cook's note: The fish you use will guide your preparation and cooking time. For cod (or any white fish) and salmon: remove any bones and cut each into 1-inch cubes. For shrimp: wash, dry, peel (including tails), and devein them. For clams: wash and scrub them clean. In general, white fish and salmon will cook at the same rate. Since these fish cook faster than the clams, be sure to add the clams first to give them a head start.

CHEF RECIPE

watch hill oyster chowder

SERVES 4

From Paul Pearson, Chef de Cuisine, Ocean House, Watch Hill, RI.

When our food forager brought in some oysters from the grower she used to work for, we decided to make chowder with them. Ocean House smokes the oysters for its famous chowder, but this version, which you can make more easily at home, is just as good.

³/₄	pound (about 10) fresh oysters
3-4	cups fish or low-sodium vegetable stock
4	slices thick-cut smoked bacon, diced
1	tablespoon unsalted butter
³/₄	cup white onion (about ¹/₂ medium onion), diced
³/₄	cup Yukon gold potato, diced into 1-inch pieces
	Pinch kosher salt
¹/₂	cup celery (about 1 large stalk), diced
¹/₂	cup flour
¹/₂	cup fresh corn kernels (from about 1 medium ear)
1	cup half and half (or cream)
	Freshly ground white pepper, to taste
	Pinch of cayenne pepper
1	lemon
1¹/₂	tablespoons chopped chives
	Crackers or crusty bread, for serving

1. Shuck oysters (for instructions, see page 124), placing in a small bowl as you go, making sure to save as much liquid as possible from each oyster. Remove oysters from bowl and place in another small bowl. Pour reserved liquid through a paper towel-lined fine mesh sieve into another bowl. Measure out oyster liquid and add enough stock to get liquid to 4 cups total. Pour liquid into a medium saucepan and place over medium-high heat.
2. Add bacon to a large saucepan and place over medium heat. Cook until bacon starts to get slight color and has rendered some fat. Remove pan from heat and add butter, followed by onions and potatoes. Return pan back to stove and increase heat to high. Add a pinch of salt. Cook until onions and potatoes are just softened, about 5 minutes. Add celery and cook for 1 minute. Add flour, stirring to coat vegetables. Cook until flour is incorporated, about 1 minute. Add stock and bring mixture to a boil. Add corn and simmer until potatoes are just tender, about 30-45 minutes.
3. Add half and half (or cream) and bring to a simmer. Cook for 4-5 minutes. Season with salt, pepper, a pinch of cayenne, and a couple drops of lemon juice. Add shucked oysters and remove from heat. Pour into warm bowls and sprinkle with chopped chives. Serve warm with crackers or crusty bread.

portuguese kale soup

SERVES 4-6

Almost every Portuguese restaurant along the southern coast of New England offers a version of this soup. What makes this soup distinctly Portuguese is the spicy sausage, either chouriço or linguiça. The soup's flavor will vary from one restaurant to another depending on the chouriço or linguiça they use. This version stays true to the essence and roots of the dish but adds diced tomatoes, which gives the soup a hearty, stew-like quality.

2   tablespoons extra virgin olive oil
2   mild chouriço (or linguiça) links, diced (or cut into half moons)
1/2 onion, finely minced
     Kosher salt, to taste
     Freshly ground black pepper, to taste
2   cloves garlic, finely minced
1   bunch curly kale, washed, stemmed, and roughly chopped (about 1-inch pieces)
2   large potatoes, peeled and diced
2   cups diced tomatoes
1   bay leaf
6-7 cups low-sodium vegetable stock

1. In a medium stock pot, heat oil over medium-high heat. Add chouriço and cook until lightly browned, about 5 minutes. Add onions and cook until softened, about 5 minutes, and season with salt and pepper. Add garlic and cook for another 1-2 minutes. Add 1 cup stock to deglaze pan, scraping browned bits from bottom of pan. Add kale, potatoes, tomatoes, bay leaf, and enough additional stock to cover vegetables, about 5 more cups. Reduce heat to simmer until kale is tender and potatoes are cooked through, about 1 hour.
2. Remove bay leaf and serve warm.

cook's note: Chouriço and linguiça are available throughout New England. However, if you can't locate chouriço or linguiça, you can substitute with a spicy Italian sausage instead.

CHOURIÇO + LINGUIÇA

All over the South Coast region you'll find chouriço and linguiça in markets and on menus. Except for a few subtle differences, these popular Portuguese sausages are surprisingly similar. Both are essentially made from the same ingredients: pork (shoulder or butt), paprika, garlic, salt, pepper, and wine, stuffed into casings. Chouriço, however, is stuffed into beef casings, while linguiça is stuffed into hog casings. Another difference is that chouriço is often a bit coarser than linguiça, but texture and fat content vary from one manufacturer to another, as does spice level. Each manufacturer has its own recipe, most of which have been passed down for generations. Debates over which sausage is spicier tend to end without a clear winner, as this too depends upon the sausage maker's preference.

You can find excellent sausages from the following sources (although local to Southern New England, all of these companies ship anywhere in the United States):

GASPAR'S SAUSAGE COMPANY, INC.

Founded in 1912, this fourth-generation company is still using the original recipe for traditional Portuguese smoked sausages that Manuel A. Gaspar brought with him when he emigrated here from Portugal. Today, Gaspar's is the largest manufacturer of Portuguese sausage in the country, producing over three million pounds each year.

MELLO'S CHOURIÇO

Mello's North End Manufacturers (Mello's Chouriço) has been in business in Southeastern Massachusetts since the early 1900s. Eduardo and Irene Rego, who met in their native Portugal, purchased it in 1978. In 1966, Irene immigrated to the United States with her family. After finishing his military duty in Portugal in 1970, Eduardo joined her in the United States. Shortly thereafter, they married and began their life together. Purchasing a small business fulfilled their American dream and allowed them to enjoy their passion for food and culture from their native land.

ACOREANA MARKET

Located in the heart of Fall River, Acoreana Market is a small, family-run Portuguese store that makes some of the best Portuguese sausage in the area. The Alden Street store, run by Maria Nunes and her brother-in-law Marcelino Aguiar, has been making their traditional, old-style sausages in the back kitchen for over thirty-two years. Walk into their shop and chances are you'll find Domingos behind the counter, ready to help you. The sausages are made fresh every day except Friday, when the store offers a Portuguese buffet for lunch instead. Acoreana Market not only stocks plenty of fresh sausage, but offers a wide range of Portuguese products and ingredients as well. Their friendly, down-home service makes it a pleasure to shop there.

chilled sweet corn soup with lobster

SERVES 4

In New England the corn season stretches from July until October, and dozens of roadside stands selling fresh corn pop up across the countryside. Cervelli Farm in Rochester, MA sells some of the sweetest corn I've ever tasted, and in the summer I frequent the farm stand quite a bit. As most New Englanders will tell you, good corn is worth the effort. This is especially true in this recipe that pairs two of the region's most popular ingredients. This chilled soup is incredibly refreshing on a hot summer day and is the perfect foundation for fresh lobster.

12 ears corn, husks and silks removed
2   tablespoons unsalted butter, divided
1   large shallot, minced
    Kosher salt, to taste
    Freshly ground black pepper, to taste
1   large clove garlic, finely minced
2   tablespoons white wine
1/4 cup heavy cream
2   lobster tails, cooked, cooled, shell removed, and cut in half, for garnish

1. Remove kernels from corn. One ear at a time, cut off end of cob and stand it straight up. With a sharp paring knife, carefully cut off corn kernels and place in a large bowl. Repeat until all but 1 ear remains. Reserve 4 cobs and set aside. Discard remaining cobs. Remove kernels from last ear of corn, place in a separate bowl, and reserve for garnish.
2. Place 4 reserved cobs and 6 cups of water in a large stockpot and bring to a boil. Cover, reduce heat to low, and cook for about 30 minutes. Remove cobs from water and discard. Keep corn stock over medium heat.
3. In a large saucepan, heat butter over medium heat. Add shallot; cook until softened, about 5 minutes, and season with salt and pepper. Add garlic and cook for another 1-2 minutes. Deglaze pan with wine, scraping browned bits from bottom of pan. Cook until wine has evaporated, about 1-2 minutes. Stir in corn kernels and cook for another 1-2 minutes. Add corn stock (if liquid doesn't cover all of kernels, add an additional 1-2 cups of water). Bring to a boil. Reduce heat to simmer, stirring occasionally, for 20-25 minutes.
4. Remove from heat and, using an immersion blender, purée until smooth (or purée soup in batches in blender). Transfer puréed soup to a large bowl. Stir in cream. If soup looks too thick, add more cream. Allow soup to cool to room temperature. Chill soup in refrigerator for at least 2 hours.
5. To serve, divide corn soup among serving bowls and place one half of a lobster tail, cut side down, in center of each bowl. Top with reserved raw corn kernels, season with salt and pepper, and serve.

CHEF RECIPE

bread + garlic soup with rhubarb compote + garden blossoms

SERVES 2-4

From Josh Lewin, Executive Chef, Beacon Hill Hotel & Bistro, Boston, MA.

This is a comforting soup that can be served either hot or cold, depending on the fickle New England spring. A few homemade croutons, a dollop of rhubarb compote, and fresh garden herbs (or even wild plants) will swim happily on top of this soup. Grains of paradise, a spice from West Africa, bring out a musky, peppery flavor in the soup and stand up to the garlic. The dried arbol chili, which is closely related to cayenne peppers, is a bright red, narrow pepper that adds a nice, smoky flavor.

You can use just about any fresh garden herbs for garnish here. For something zingy: garden sorrel, oxalis, or purslane; for something deeply flavored: nettles or goosefoot; for something assertive: young mustard greens, watercress, or nasturtium flowers.

Rhubarb Compote
2 cups sugar
2½ cups water
12 sprigs fresh oregano
1 pound rhubarb, cut into 1-inch pieces

¼ cup day-old bread (crusts removed), finely diced
2 tablespoons unsalted butter
1 whole head fresh garlic, peeled and crushed
3 large shallots, sliced
1 dried arbol chile
1 teaspoon ground grains of paradise
   Kosher salt
12 sprigs fresh thyme
4 sprigs fresh rosemary
2 fresh bay leaves
1 teaspoon black peppercorns
½ teaspoon whole coriander seeds
2 cups day-old bread (crusts removed), diced
1 cup dry white wine
4 cups (homemade) chicken stock
   Juice from ½ lemon
   Garden blossoms, for garnish (see headnote)

1. Make rhubarb compote. Place sugar, water, and oregano in a medium saucepan and place over medium heat. Bring to a boil and cook for about 2 minutes until sugar is dissolved. Remove from heat and allow to cool. Remove oregano and transfer syrup to refrigerator until cold.
2. Place cold syrup in a stainless steel saucepan and add rhubarb. Cover and bring to a boil. Simmer for 1 minute. Remove from heat and allow mixture to cool to room temperature. Set aside.
3. Make croutons (for garnish). Place finely diced bread on a baking sheet and place under broiler. Toast until golden brown, about 1-2 minutes. Set aside.
4. In a heavy-bottomed saucepan, melt butter over medium-low heat. Add garlic, shallots, arbol chili, grains of paradise, and a good pinch of salt and sweat for 5 minutes (be careful not to allow mixture to burn or brown at all as it will turn results bitter).
5. Meanwhile, place thyme, rosemary, bay leaves, peppercorns, and coriander seeds in a cheesecloth and tie with twine, making a sachet. Set aside.
6. Add diced bread to saucepan with garlic and continue to sweat until garlic and shallots are completely softened and bread is beginning to break down. Add wine and cook until nearly dry. Add chicken stock and sachet of herbs to saucepan and slowly bring to a boil. Reduce heat to simmer until bread is completely broken down, about 8-10 minutes. Remove sachet and arbol chile and discard both.
7. Transfer soup to a blender and purée until completely smooth. Add lemon juice and taste for seasoning.
8. Divide soup among serving bowls and top with some toasted breadcrumbs and a small dollop of rhubarb compote. Garnish with fresh picked garden blossoms and serve.

steamed clams in garlic, lemon + beer broth

SERVES 4

Clamming in New England is a summer ritual. It is a primal, rejuvenating experience that appeals to Yankee sensibilities from Maine to Connecticut. Coastal New Englanders will spend the better portion of their summers covered in mud, wading about the shallows, looking for clams. This recipe is an easy and flavorful way to enjoy that bounty. While most light-bodied beers complement this recipe well, Sam Adams Summer Ale is a good choice here, as it plays off the hints of lemon in the broth.

2   dozen littleneck clams
2   tablespoons unsalted butter
2   cloves garlic, finely minced
    Kosher salt, to taste
    Freshly ground black pepper, to taste
1   12-ounce bottle of beer (see headnote)
1   lemon, cut into thin slices
1   lemon, cut into wedges, for serving
2   tablespoons finely minced fresh flat-leaf Italian
    parsley, for serving
1   French baguette, for serving

1. Check clams and make sure none are already open. If any are open, gently push shells together with your fingers to see if clams will close. If they don't, discard. Wash clams one at a time under running water, removing any sand with your fingers or a small brush, and set aside.
2. In a large saucepan, add butter over medium heat. Add garlic and cook until just fragrant, about 1-2 minutes (do not let it burn or turn brown), and season with salt and pepper. Add beer and lemon slices and bring to slow boil. Add clams. Increase heat to high, cover, and continue to cook until clams open, about 5-10 minutes. Discard any unopened clams. Divide clams equally among serving bowls.
3. Strain clam broth through a fine-mesh sieve. Divide strained broth among serving bowls. Add a lemon wedge to each bowl and top with some parsley. Serve warm with bread.

roasted butternut squash soup with maple cream

SERVES 4

Ever since I was a kid in Vermont, I have loved the changing seasons in New England, watching the leaves shift from one vibrant hue to the next. When the days start to cool, I yearn for large bowls of warm soup. This one is my favorite way to enjoy butternut squash.

1   large butternut squash, peeled, seeded,
      and diced (see cook's note)
1   small yellow onion, diced
2   tablespoons extra virgin olive oil
      Kosher salt, to taste
      Freshly ground black pepper, to taste
4-5   cups low-sodium vegetable stock
1/4   cup heavy cream
1/4   cup sour cream
1 1/2 teaspoons maple syrup, plus extra
      for drizzling

1. Preheat oven to 425°F.
2. Place squash and onions on a large baking sheet, toss with olive oil, and season with salt and pepper. Roast until vegetables are lightly browned on all sides and softened, about 35-40 minutes.
3. Transfer squash and onion mixture to a large saucepan along with 2 cups of stock. Using an immersion blender, purée until smooth. (Or purée soup in batches with 2 cups of stock in blender and transfer back to saucepan once puréed.) Add another 2 cups of stock and cream. Stir to combine. Stir in more stock until soup reaches desired consistency. Simmer until soup is heated through, about 10 minutes.
4. In a small bowl, combine sour cream and maple syrup. Ladle soup into bowls and top each with a spoonful of maple cream. Drizzle some additional maple syrup over top of each and serve warm.

cook's note: Squash seeds make a nice, crunchy garnish. Once removed, wash and dry 1/4 cup seeds. Place on a baking sheet and roast at 425°F until golden brown, about 5 minutes. Season with salt while warm.

garden carrot soup

SERVES 2-4

Carrots are one of those rare New England crops that are readily available at farmers' markets nearly all year long, making them an ideal ingredient for all varieties of soup. This one, however, is perfect for those early autumn afternoons when the air begins to cool and you need something luxurious to warm you up. The carrot greens add a beautiful—though slightly bitter—garnish, so it's best to pair them with something milder, like parsley.

2 tablespoons extra virgin olive oil
1 large shallot, diced
   Kosher salt, to taste
   Freshly ground black pepper, to taste
4 large carrots, peeled, trimmed, and diced
6-7 cups low-sodium vegetable stock
1/4 cup heavy cream, plus extra for serving
2 tablespoons finely minced carrot greens, for garnish
2 tablespoons finely minced fresh flat-leaf Italian parsley, for garnish

1. In a large saucepan, heat olive oil over medium heat. Add shallot and cook until translucent, about 3 minutes. Season with salt and pepper. Add carrots and enough stock to cover vegetables, about 5 cups, and bring to a boil. Reduce heat to simmer until vegetables are tender and you can easily pierce carrots with a fork, about 40 minutes.
2. Remove from heat and, using an immersion blender, purée until smooth, adding more stock as needed. (Or purée soup in batches in blender and transfer back to saucepan once puréed.) Stir in cream. Simmer until warmed through, about 5-10 minutes. Stir in more stock until soup reaches desired consistency.
3. Make garnish. Remove leafy fronds (not thicker stem) from 1 carrot top and finely mince, then toss with minced parsley.
4. Ladle soup into serving bowls. Pour a small amount of cream onto a teaspoon and carefully add to center of each bowl. To make a decorative swirl, drag a toothpick through cream. Place a small amount of greens on top of each bowl and serve warm.

egg salad tartine with breakfast radishes + chives

SERVES 4

When the farmers' markets open in the spring, I look for radishes. Few other vegetables seem as charming and vibrant, and they just beckon me to take them home. When I can find them, French breakfast radishes are my first choice. They are a touch milder than regular radishes, with an oblong shape and hues that taper from scarlet to white. They add a nice crunch to salads and make great snacks on their own. They are also stunning atop a simple sandwich like this French tartine.

4 extra large eggs
2 tablespoons mayonnaise
2 tablespoons Dijon mustard
   Kosher salt, to taste
   Freshly ground black pepper, to taste
1 teaspoon finely minced fresh chives, or to taste
4 1/2-inch thick slices sourdough (or country) bread, toasted
2-3 breakfast radishes, thinly sliced
4 chive stems, ends trimmed and cut in half, for garnish

1. Place eggs in a saucepan and fill with enough cold water to cover eggs by about 1 inch. Bring to a gentle boil; remove from heat. Cover and let stand for 12 minutes. Drain and rinse eggs with cold water. Let stand for 5 minutes, then peel eggs.
2. Coarsely chop eggs and add to a medium bowl. Add mayonnaise and mustard, season with salt and pepper, and stir to combine. Gently stir in minced chives. Divide egg salad equally over bread slices, covering entire surface of each slice evenly with egg salad. Top each with a few slices of radish and season with salt. Place two chive stems in an "x" pattern over top of each for garnish and serve.

cook's note: If you can't find French breakfast radishes, substitute with another variety.

serrano + manchego sandwich with quince

SERVES 4

Quince spread is a pale, orange jelly that's made from cooked quinces, which grow locally and are in season in the late fall. Making a quince jelly can be an involved process. Thankfully, it's readily available at most gourmet markets. It's firmer than most jellies but is still spreadable, and pairs perfectly with Manchego cheese in this really simple, Spanish-inspired sandwich that is great after a morning on the water or for a seaside picnic.

1   French baguette
4   tablespoons Dijon mustard
4   tablespoons quince spread
    Spanish olive oil (or any good olive oil),
    for drizzling
    Kosher salt, to taste
    Freshly ground black pepper, to taste
8   slices Manchego cheese
8   thin slices Serrano ham

1. Cut baguette in half lengthwise. Spread mustard on bottom half and spread quince jelly on top half.
2. Drizzle mustard side of bread with a little bit of olive oil and season with salt and pepper. Top with Manchego cheese, evenly covering top of bread, followed by Serrano ham.
3. Fold top half of bread over and press lightly to close. Cut into 4 equal sandwiches and serve immediately, or wrap in parchment until ready to serve.

tuna niçoise sandwich with crumbled eggs + tomatoes

SERVES 4

Any time I'm in a little French bistro, I always end up ordering a niçoise salad. I love the combination of flavors. Here, the elements of this classic salad—fresh poached tuna, briny olives, and creamy eggs—prove they are just as good when served on a crusty baguette.

4   extra large eggs
1   pound fresh tuna

Vinaigrette
1   clove garlic, finely minced
1   tablespoon Dijon mustard
1   tablespoon red wine vinegar
    Juice from 1/2 lemon
    Kosher salt, to taste
    Freshly ground black pepper, to taste
1/4 cup extra virgin olive oil

1   French baguette, cut in half lengthwise
1   small red onion, thinly sliced
2   tomatoes, thinly sliced
1/4 cup prepared black olive tapenade

1. Place eggs in a saucepan and fill with enough cold water to cover eggs by about 1 inch. Bring to a gentle boil; remove from heat. Cover and let stand for 12 minutes. Drain and rinse eggs with cold water. Let stand for 5 minutes, and then peel eggs. Roughly chop and set aside.
2. Meanwhile, place tuna in a large saucepan and fill with enough water to cover tuna by about 1 inch. Bring to a gentle simmer (do not boil) until fish is cooked through and can be easily flaked apart, about 10-12 minutes. Remove from water (avoiding any skim that might have formed on top), transfer to a bowl, and allow to cool. Using a fork, gently separate tuna into big flakes. Set aside.
3. Make vinaigrette. In a small bowl, combine garlic, mustard, vinegar, and lemon juice and season with salt and pepper. Slowly whisk in olive oil to emulsify until vinaigrette is thickened. Set aside.
4. Hollow out bottom piece of bread by removing some of its interior from entire half of bread, making a well (discard or save for another use). Brush vinaigrette evenly into hollowed out area of bread with a pastry brush, allowing bread to soak it up. Fill evenly with chopped eggs, followed by a layer of tuna. Top with a layer of red onions followed by tomatoes, evenly covering entire half of bread. Spread top half of bread with tapenade and place on top of bottom half of bread, closing up sandwich. Carefully press it together. Cut sandwich into 4 equal pieces and serve immediately, or wrap in parchment until ready to serve.

cook's note: This preparation of poaching the tuna cooks it all the way through, but if you prefer, you can also lightly sear the tuna and slice it thin for the sandwich.

THREE UNIQUE AND CHARMING LUNCH SPOTS
THAT ARE WORTH THE TRIP:

ANSEL S. GURNEY HOUSE

Tucked away in Marion, MA, the Ansel S. Gurney House has been in business for over thirty-five years. This family-owned store is a treasure trove for cooks and food enthusiasts. The historic home, the oldest part of which dates to the 1700s, is filled with everything from housewares to picnic baskets to cookbooks. The Gunschel family purchased the home in the 1930s and raised three sons there; in 1976 they turned their home into a gift shop and restaurant.

After spending a few hours browsing inside, be sure to stop by the café for a bite. Daily offerings include seasonal soups, salads, sandwiches, and a wide selection of desserts, all made on location. Be prepared to lose hours here, shopping, dining, and strolling through the family's extensive outdoor gardens.

HOW ON EARTH

Located in Mattapoisett, MA, How On Earth sells local and organic grocery items, including seasonal fruits and vegetables, dairy, eggs, meat, breads, jams, honey, and herbs, as well as items in bulk. Lunch in the café features items made from local ingredients, and prepared foods are available for takeout. Be sure to save room for something sweet, though. Flour Girls Baking Co. sells its cookies and bars right at the checkout counter and they are not to be missed (you can also visit the new Flour Girls Baking Co. store in Fairhaven, MA). These locally made treats by Jill Houck are to die for—especially the oversized ginger molasses cookies.

PARTNERS VILLAGE STORE & KITCHEN

Since 1979, Partners Village Store & Kitchen has been one of the South Coast's most inviting destinations. The shop, which is located on Main Road in Westport, MA, includes a unique selection of gifts, toys, specialty foods, and paper goods, all with an emphasis on the local community. Its intimate bookshop is the perfect place to browse works from local writers and national authors. Partners also offers tempting treats from its kitchen, where you'll find an ever-changing array of homemade (and ridiculously good) muffins, scones, and giant cookies. Partners also has daily offerings of soups and sandwiches. It's a great place to spend time browsing for those perfect little treasures you didn't know you needed.

from the garden

lemon verbena sun tea

roasted beet salad with goat cheese + pistachios

lemon cucumber + radish salad

russian kale + apple salad

spring pasta with asparagus + poached egg

cloumage pizza with garden greens

raw corn salad with lime vinaigrette

quinoa tabbouleh with garden cucumbers

rustic mediterranean panzanella

brussels sprouts salad with apples

green bean salad with dijon vinaigrette

green salad with fresh herb vinaigrette + chive blossoms

creamed summer corn

roasted zucchini + summer squash salad with creamy basil vinaigrette

free-form garden lasagna

zucchini ribbons with creamy goat cheese dressing

simple year-round tomato sauce

heirloom tomatoes with feta + olives

smashed potato salad

The coast of Southeastern Massachusetts and Rhode Island is known as the Farm Coast for a reason. It's here where the region's picture-perfect villages and fertile farmland meet the sea, combining to produce some of the very best food in New England—and possibly in the country.

While much of New England is rich in small farms, there is something magical here, where farms framed by ancient stone walls stretch across foggy peninsulas and alongside grassy salt marshes. But it's more than just a pretty place. The climate here is also exceptionally suitable to growing a wide range of produce. The warm waters of Narragansett and Buzzards bays keep the temperatures mild and the air moist, ensuring a longer growing season. Rich soil and a flat coastal landscape are also factors that make our farms some of New England's best.

Many of us are dedicated gardeners as well, happy to shake off the cold, wet winters and see what our little patches of dirt can yield each season. This section provides recipes that will make the most of the amazing produce you can find at your local farm stand—or to celebrate what you have growing in your own backyard.

lemon verbena sun tea

SERVES 4-6

Lemon verbena is a small herb plant with shiny, delicate leaves. It's a great plant to have in your container garden, as it is an easy way to add a subtle hint of lemon to a dish or drink. You can find these plants at farmers' markets or garden centers during the summer months. Here, a splash of infused simple syrup is the perfect addition to a refreshing glass of sun tea on a hot summer day.

Lemon Verbena Simple Syrup

$1/2$ cup granulated sugar
$1/2$ cup cold water
6-8 sprigs of fresh lemon verbena, divided

1 quart prepared (or homemade) iced sun tea
1 lemon, thinly sliced
    Ice, for serving

1. Make simple syrup. In a small saucepan, add sugar, water, and 2 sprigs lemon verbena and bring to a boil. Stir until sugar dissolves. Remove from heat, cover, and steep simple syrup for 10 minutes. Cool to room temperature. Remove lemon verbena and discard. Refrigerate simple syrup until ready to use (syrup will keep for up to 2 weeks in your refrigerator).
2. Fill serving glasses with ice. Add 1 tablespoon of chilled lemon verbena simple syrup to each glass. Divide iced sun tea among glasses and stir. Taste for sweetness and add more simple syrup if desired. Add a fresh sprig of lemon verbena and a slice of lemon to each glass for garnish and serve.

cook's note: To make sun tea, steep 4 to 6 tea bags in a 2 quart glass container filled with water. Place container in sun for 3 to 5 hours. When the tea has reached desired strength, remove from sun and refrigerate until cool. Remove tea bags before serving.

roasted beet salad with goat cheese + pistachios

SERVES 4

When roasted, beets transform into sweet purple gems that pop off a plate of simple garden greens. Topped with creamy, white goat cheese and flecks of crunchy green pistachios, this dish is full of texture and vibrant colors that can brighten up even the dreariest day.

2 large beets, greens and stems removed, washed and dried
1 tablespoon white wine vinegar
    Juice from $1/2$ orange
    Kosher salt, to taste
    Freshly ground black pepper, to taste
$1/4$ cup extra virgin olive oil
3 cups mixed salad greens (such as mesclun), washed and dried
4 ounces goat cheese, softened
$1/4$ cup shelled pistachios, roughly chopped

1. Preheat oven to 400°F.
2. Wrap whole, unpeeled beets in aluminum foil and place on a baking sheet. Roast until beets can be easily pierced with a fork, about 45-55 minutes. Unwrap and allow them to cool. When cool enough to handle, carefully pull off skins and discard. Cut off ends and slice beets into large wedges.
3. Make vinaigrette. In a small bowl, combine vinegar and orange juice and season with salt and pepper. Slowly add olive oil and mix until well combined.
4. Place salad greens down center of a large serving platter. Place wedges of beets around outside of platter. Crumble goat cheese over top of salad and scatter pistachios over top of cheese. Drizzle entire platter with vinaigrette, season with salt and pepper, and serve immediately.

cook's note: Save the leftover beet greens. They can be sautéed and served as a side dish, cooked with eggs for a quick breakfast, or added to a batch of homemade vegetable stock.

lemon cucumber + radish salad

SERVES 2-4

Lemon cucumbers are about the size of a lemon and have a yellow exterior when ripe. The name comes from their appearance, not their flavor. They are one of the easiest cucumbers to grow in your vegetable garden, but pick them while they are small or they may become too seedy and lose their flavor. You can eat lemon cucumbers with the skins on, but when they're straight from the garden they tend to have tiny prickles, so I prefer them peeled. With their pleasant taste, they can be used in almost any recipe that calls for cucumbers, such as this refreshing salad that has a tangy vinaigrette and plenty of satisfying crunch.

2   cups baby arugula, washed and dried
1/4 cup roughly chopped fresh flat-leaf
     Italian parsley
1-2 lemon cucumbers, peeled and sliced
4-5 radishes, thinly sliced

Lemon Vinaigrette
1   tablespoon Dijon mustard
     Juice from 1 lemon
     Kosher salt, to taste
     Freshly ground black pepper, to taste
1/4 cup extra virgin olive oil

4   ounces feta cheese, crumbled

1. In a large serving bowl, add arugula, parsley, cucumber, and radish.
2. Make vinaigrette. In a small bowl, combine mustard and lemon juice and season with salt and pepper. Slowly whisk in olive oil to emulsify. Pour enough vinaigrette over salad to coat.
3. Top with feta cheese and serve immediately.

russian kale + apple salad

SERVES 2-4

In the summer, when there is a wide variety of kale available at the farmers' markets, I always look for white or red Russian kale from Arcadian Fields (based in Hope Valley, RI). These varieties of kale have a more delicate leaf, are slightly milder in taste, and are a great choice during the warmer months when you want something light and healthy. It's important to let the salad sit at room temperature for about 10 minutes so that the kale softens just a bit before serving.

1   medium Granny Smith apple
     Juice from 1 lemon
3-4 tablespoons extra virgin olive oil
     Kosher salt, to taste
     Freshly ground black pepper, to taste
1   bunch white or red Russian kale, washed
     and dried

1. Cut apple into thin slices and then julienne, cutting into matchsticks. Place in a large bowl and toss with lemon juice and 2 tablespoons olive oil. Season with salt and pepper, making sure all of apple slices are well coated, and set aside.
2. Trim bottoms of kale leaves and discard. Remove and discard stems and cut or tear kale leaves into large bite-size pieces, about 2-inches in size.
3. Add kale to bowl with apple and gently toss to combine. Allow to sit at room temperature for about 10 minutes. Toss with additional olive oil (if needed) just before serving.

cook's note: Toasted walnuts and/or crumbled blue cheese are wonderful savory additions to the salad.

spring pasta with asparagus + poached egg

SERVES 4

A natural affinity exists between eggs and asparagus—especially when paired in this fresh and simple pasta dish. Local asparagus comes into the markets in late April, making this dish one of my springtime favorites. As there are so few ingredients, it's important to use the freshest asparagus and eggs possible (the fresher the eggs, the better they will set when poaching). A combination of purple and green microgreens on top adds a burst of color and contrast to this delicious, wholesome dish.

1   bunch fresh asparagus, ends trimmed and
      cut on a diagonal into 2-inch pieces
1   pound spaghetti

Lemon Vinaigrette
1 1/2 tablespoons Dijon mustard
      Juice from 2 lemons
      Kosher salt, to taste
      Freshly ground black pepper, to taste
1/4 cup extra virgin olive oil, plus extra for drizzling

4   extra large eggs
2   teaspoons distilled vinegar
1   cup mixed microgreens (greens and purples),
      for garnish, washed and dried

1. Bring a large pot of water to boil. Add asparagus and blanch until bright green, about 3-5 minutes (depending on thickness of asparagus stalks). Remove with a slotted spoon and place in a bowl of ice water to shock and cool. Keep pot of water boiling on stove.
2. To boiling water, add a good pinch of salt. Add pasta and cook until al dente, about 7-10 minutes.
3. Meanwhile, make vinaigrette. In a medium bowl, combine mustard and lemon juice and season with salt and pepper. Slowly pour in olive oil, whisking until thick and emulsified.
4. Fill a shallow pot with water, coming up about 2 inches on side of pan. Bring to a boil. Lower heat so that water is just barely boiling. Add vinegar to water.
5. Crack each egg into its own small bowl. (This will

make it easier to transfer eggs to water.) Add one egg into water, taking care not to break yolk. Wait 1 minute, and then add another egg, adding all 4 in same manner. (Do this in batches if your pan isn't large enough to hold all of them at once.) Allow each egg to cook until whites are set, just about 2 minutes (yolks should still be runny). Carefully remove each egg with a slotted spoon in same order each was added, allowing excess water to drain off. Place eggs on a large plate.
6. When asparagus has cooled, drain and pat completely dry. Set aside.
7. Drain and transfer pasta to a medium bowl. Toss warm pasta with 1/2 of vinaigrette. Divide pasta among serving bowls and top each with equal amount of asparagus. Place one egg atop each bowl followed by a handful of microgreens. Drizzle top of each serving bowl with remaining vinaigrette. Season with salt and pepper and serve.

cook's note: The addition of either feta, goat cheese, or a dusting of good Parmigiano-Reggiano is especially delicious.

cloumage pizza with garden greens

SERVES 4-6

Cloumage is a fresh artisanal cheese curd created and produced locally by Shy Brothers Farm in Westport, MA (see page 57). With a taste reminiscent of a creamy goat cheese and a texture similar to ricotta, it makes for a perfectly elegant spread on grilled pizza. Fresh lemon and garden greens scattered over the top are all you need to complete this easy appetizer, ideal for summer entertaining.

Cloumage Spread
1   cup Cloumage
    Zest and juice from 1 lemon
    Kosher salt, to taste
    Freshly ground black pepper, to taste

    Flour, for dusting
1   prepared pizza dough, cut in half
    (see page 135)
2   tablespoons extra virgin olive oil, plus extra
    for serving
1   cup fresh garden greens (such as microgreens
    or baby arugula), washed and dried

1. Preheat grill to medium-high heat.
2. Make Cloumage spread. In a small bowl, combine Cloumage, lemon zest, and juice. Season with salt and pepper. Set aside.
3. On a lightly floured surface, gently stretch each dough half into a rectangle, approximately 4 x 12 inches in size. Brush both sides of each piece of dough with olive oil and season one side of each with salt and pepper. Place each piece of dough onto grill, seasoned side down (or cook one at a time) and cook until lightly charred on bottom, about 3-4 minutes. Flip each piece of dough and grill on other side until lightly charred, another 3-4 minutes.
4. Transfer grilled dough onto a large cutting board. Smear top of each dough with equal parts of Cloumage spread. Scatter greens over top of each. Season with salt and pepper and drizzle with a bit of olive oil. Cut into pieces and serve.

cooks note: Either fresh ricotta or goat cheese is a suitable alternative to Cloumage. It's important to use smaller pieces of dough when grilling pizza so that they are easier to flip.

shy brothers farm, westport, ma

The Santos brothers, two sets of fraternal twins who are third-generation dairy farmers, own Shy Brothers Farm. Arthur and Norman are the older set of twins, and Kevin and Karl are the younger. This extremely shy band of brothers (hence the name) are quietly producing some of the best artisanal cheese in New England.

The farm is located on the highest land on a peninsula between two branches of the Westport River. Because of its position, the farm experiences cool gentle breezes in the summer and moderate temperatures in the winter. As a result, the farm's 120 milking cows (Holstein, Ayrshire, and Jersey) are able to stay at pasture longer than other cows in the region. The unique characteristics of the farm's soil, grass, climate, and proximity to the ocean play a role in the flavors of the milk and the resulting cheese.

Cheesemaking wasn't always the plan for the brothers. But back in 2006, when dropping milk prices forced neighboring dairy farms to go out of business, the brothers faced the unthinkable prospect of losing their 125-acre family farm. They took a hard look at their business and knew they needed to make some changes. With the help of friends Barbara Hanley and Leo Brooks, they decided to begin producing their own artisanal cheeses.

Barbara and Leo accompanied Karl to France, where he learned as much as he could about cheesemaking. The group wanted something different, something that wasn't readily available in the United States. They found a recipe for *bouton de culotte*, or "trouser buttons." While *bouton de culotte* are typically made from goat's milk and are somewhat dry and salty, Karl decided to make them with cow's milk. The result has come to be known as Hannahbells, named after their mother, Hannah, as well as the small thimble, bell-like shape of the cheese.

The process to produce Hannahbells is labor intensive, and it takes ten days to make a single batch of ten thousand. Each morning before the sun comes up, Norman milks the cows. Karl then carefully pasteurizes the milk to protect the natural enzymes. When the milk reaches the exact temperature needed to obtain the cheese's signature creaminess, Karl adds imported cultures and natural rennet. After a week of careful attention, he moves the thimbles into the ripening room, where they mature for a few more days. The brothers make all of the cheese the old-fashioned way, letting the milk and cultures do the work. No heat, no pressing, no hurrying. The wonderful flavors develop all on their own.

These delightful little thimbles are found on the menus of some of New England's best restaurants and are available in gourmet markets across the region. But the brothers haven't stopped there. In 2009, they introduced Cloumage, an artisanal curd based on a classic French recipe. The curd is formed using a long, slow acidification process, and is then allowed to drain naturally under its own weight. The resulting texture is light and fluffy—similar to a ricotta. Cloumage is perfect as a simple spread with figs and honey, in savory tarts, or layered into desserts.

With a very loyal following and as winners of several regional and international awards, it appears that the Santos brothers made the right decision to enter the world of cheesemaking.

NORTHSTAR FARM

While there is no shortage of amazing farms along the southern coast of New England, only a few like NorthStar Farm make the commitment to grow through the winter season. It's a big investment, which is why most farmers can't do it. Those who do, however, find their winter produce in high demand.

NorthStar Farm is run by Steve Hancock, who bought the farm in 2006 after working on the property as the head perennials grower. With such a competitive wholesale perennials market and short sales season, he began to grow in the winter to keep the farm profitable all year long. Winter salad greens and spinach were their first crops. Since that time, he has added sweet potatoes, carrots, root vegetables, zucchini, summer squash, and kale—to name a few. Keep your eyes open for NorthStar Farm at the growing array of winter farmers' markets around the area.

FOUR TOWN FARM

Four Town Farm is a 150-acre farm located at the junction of Seekonk, MA, Swansea, MA, Barrington, RI and East Providence, RI run by the Clegg Family. Now in its fifth generation, the farm attributes its long success to the many family members who worked there over the years.

Four Town Farm originally began as a wholesale operation, selling produce to supermarkets, but in 1972, it introduced a farm stand and began selling directly to the public. The farm stand has grown into one of the area's most popular destinations for fresh fruits and vegetables in the area; and the farm's extensive pick-your-own crop selection, which includes English peas, fava beans, strawberries, raspberries, and pumpkins, make this a perfect place for families to visit as well.

Four Town Farm is a family business through and through. Chris Clegg, who works with his father and uncle, now runs the farm. His mother runs the greenhouses, and his aunt runs the retail stand, which is their primary sales outlet (they also sell wholesale to local restaurants through Farm Fresh Rhode Island). All of the family members have worked on the farm since they were young children, learning the trade from an early age.

What helps set Four Town Farm apart is its strong attention to how it farms. The farm cultivates a broad array of crops and takes care to rotate where each is planted. To take it a step further, crops that are past the point of picking are remixed into the soil to help fortify it. Chris takes careful measures to reduce the amounts of pesticides used, using only the safest and most organic ones when necessary.

Running any farm is hard work, but the years of knowledge and experience passed down from one generation to another have helped make Four Town Farm efficient and a favorite in the area.

raw corn salad with lime vinaigrette

SERVES 4

New England's summer corn is so sweet that it doesn't need a lot to enhance it. Here, a simple vinaigrette of lime juice, your favorite local honey, and a hint of cumin is tossed with the raw corn kernels and fresh cilantro, making a quick side dish that pairs well with just about anything from the grill. It's a perfect light snack on its own or served alongside my backyard bbq chicken (see page 130).

8   ears of corn, husks and silks removed

Lime Vinaigrette
    Juice from 2 limes
2   tablespoons local honey
1   teaspoon ground cumin
    Kosher salt, to taste
    Freshly ground black pepper, to taste
1/4 cup extra virgin olive oil

1/4 cup finely chopped fresh cilantro

1. Remove kernels from each ear of corn. One ear at a time, cut off end of cob and stand it straight up. With a sharp paring knife, carefully cut off corn kernels from cob and place in a large bowl.
2. Make vinaigrette. In a medium bowl, combine lime juice, 1 tablespoon honey, and cumin and season with salt and pepper. Whisk in olive oil until incorporated. Taste for flavor (if it seems too tart, whisk in additional 1 tablespoon honey).
3. Pour vinaigrette over corn and toss well, coating kernels. Toss with fresh cilantro and serve immediately.

cook's note: If you're not sure your corn is sweet enough right off the cob, or if it's a little out of season, marinate the kernels in the vinaigrette for up to 1 hour. Toss with cilantro right before serving.

quinoa tabbouleh with garden cucumbers

SERVES 4

This updated version of a Middle Eastern classic, which is typically made with bulgur, uses quinoa instead. Using quinoa gives this light and easy salad a healthy punch, as it is one of the most protein-packed grains available. Be sure to toss the quinoa with olive oil and lemon juice while the quinoa is still warm so the grain absorbs the flavor. Garden cucumbers are the stars of the show here, so pick them as fresh as you can; their sweet flavor adds a crisp bite to this simple summer side dish.

1½ cups quinoa, rinsed
3   cups water
2   tablespoons extra virgin olive oil
    Juice of 1-2 lemons, divided
    Kosher salt, to taste
    Freshly ground black pepper, to taste
1   pint cherry tomatoes, cut in half
1   large cucumber, peeled, seeded, and diced
3   scallions, white and light green parts, finely diced
1/4 cup finely diced red onion
1/4 cup chopped fresh flat-leaf Italian parsley
1/4 cup chopped fresh mint

1. In a medium saucepan, bring quinoa and water to a boil. Reduce heat to low and place a cover on top of pot, slightly ajar, for about 2 minutes, until water settles down (so it doesn't overflow). Once it settles, cover completely and simmer until grains are translucent and germ ring is visible, about 10-15 minutes. Transfer to a large bowl and immediately toss with olive oil and juice from 1/2 lemon. Season with salt and pepper and allow mixture to cool to room temperature.
2. Add tomatoes, cucumber, scallions, onion, parsley, and mint to cooled quinoa and gently toss to combine. Toss with juice from 1/2 lemon and season with salt and pepper. Taste for seasoning; add more lemon juice if necessary. Serve at room temperature or chilled.

rustic mediterranean panzanella

SERVES 2-4

This panzanella, or bread salad, is a mouth-watering way to use up day-old bread and showcase tomatoes at the height of the season. My version gains its Mediterranean flavors from the feta cheese, olives, oregano, and grilled bread. Traditionally, the bread in a panzanella is supposed to sit for a bit, soaking up the liquid from the dressing, but I like my bread to have a little crunch, so I serve this dish as soon as it comes together.

1   French baguette
1/4 cup extra virgin olive oil, plus extra for drizzling
1   pint cherry tomatoes, larger ones cut in half
1   small red onion, thinly sliced
1/2 cup pitted black olives
2-4 tablespoons red wine vinegar
    Kosher salt, to taste
    Freshly ground black pepper, to taste
2   tablespoons hand-torn fresh oregano
4   ounces feta cheese

1. Preheat grill to medium heat.
2. Cut baguette in half and save one half for later use. Cut remaining baguette horizontally, making 2 pieces. Brush cut sides of bread with olive oil. Grill bread, cut sides down, until lightly charred, about 3-4 minutes. Turn bread over and grill on other side for another 1-2 minutes. Once cooled, cut bread into 1-inch cubes and set aside.
3. Meanwhile, in a large bowl, add tomatoes, red onion, and olives.
4. In a small bowl, whisk 2 tablespoons vinegar and olive oil and season with salt and pepper. Taste for flavor and add more vinegar if desired.
5. Add bread to bowl of tomatoes. Pour dressing over salad and gently toss. Add oregano and toss again. Transfer to a large serving platter and top with feta cheese. Season with salt and pepper and serve immediately.

cook's note: If you don't want to grill your bread, you can easily toast it in the oven. Simply cut bread into 1-inch cubes and place on a baking sheet. Bake at 400°F until golden brown, turning occasionally, for about 10-15 minutes.

brussels sprouts salad with apples

SERVES 4

Autumn brings an abundance of Brussels sprouts to the markets. If you've never tried Brussels sprouts raw, you may be surprised. Allowing them to marinate for a few minutes in the vinaigrette will round out their slightly bitter flavor. The addition of crunchy apples, walnuts, and tart sherry vinaigrette make this a crisp and refreshing salad.

16 large (or 20 medium) Brussels sprouts

Sherry Vinaigrette
1   medium shallot, finely minced
2   teaspoons local honey, or to taste
    Kosher salt, to taste
    Freshly ground black pepper, to taste
2   tablespoons sherry vinegar, or to taste
2   tablespoons extra virgin olive oil

2   medium McIntosh apples, diced
1/4 cup roughly chopped toasted walnuts
2   tablespoons finely minced fresh flat-leaf Italian parsley
1/4 cup crumbled blue cheese, or to taste, optional

1. Cut core end off each Brussels sprout and discard. Discard first few outer leaves as well. Cut Brussels sprouts in half, place flat side down on a cutting board and thinly slice. Place in a large bowl and set aside.
2. Make vinaigrette. In a medium bowl, combine shallot, honey, and sherry vinegar and season with salt and pepper. Slowly pour in olive oil, whisking constantly to emulsify. Taste for seasoning and adjust if necessary (add in more honey if too tart, or more sherry vinegar if too sweet).
3. Pour half of vinaigrette over Brussels sprouts and toss well to coat. Allow to sit for 5 minutes.
4. Add apples, walnuts, and parsley to bowl of Brussels sprouts. Lightly coat salad with additional vinaigrette and gently toss to combine. Transfer to a large serving platter, scatter blue cheese over top (if using), and serve immediately.

green bean salad with dijon vinaigrette

SERVES 4-6

This is one of my favorite dishes to make during green bean season, which in New England lasts all summer and well into the fall. I pair fresh, slightly crisp green beans with yellow and red tomatoes, making this salad a bright and colorful addition to the table. The tart Dijon vinaigrette provides a nice tangy bite, and it's a gorgeous dish to serve guests.

Dijon Vinaigrette
- 2   tablespoons minced shallots (about 1/2 medium shallot)
- 1   tablespoon Dijon mustard
- 1   tablespoon red wine vinegar
      Kosher salt, to taste
      Freshly ground black pepper, to taste
- 1   teaspoon finely chopped fresh thyme
- 1/4 cup extra virgin olive oil

- 1   pound green beans, trimmed
- 2   12-ounce containers red and yellow cherry tomatoes (larger ones cut in half)
- 2   heads frisée lettuce, washed and dried
      Handful fresh flat-leaf Italian parsley, roughly chopped

1. Make Dijon vinaigrette. In a medium bowl, combine shallots, mustard, and red wine vinegar and season with salt and pepper. Add thyme. Slowly whisk in olive oil to emulsify. Taste for seasonings and adjust as desired. Set aside.
2. Fill a medium saucepan with water and bring to a boil. Add green beans and cook until bright green but still have a little snap to them, about 2-3 minutes. Remove with a slotted spoon and place in a bowl of ice water to shock and cool for about 5 minutes. Drain well and pat dry. Transfer to a large bowl along with tomatoes.
3. Cut off and discard core ends of frisée. Cut or tear lettuce into bite-size pieces and add to bowl of green beans.
4. Slowly pour enough vinaigrette to lightly coat and gently toss everything together. Transfer to a serving platter, top with parsley, and serve.

EVA'S GARDEN

Eva Sommaripa is the region's most notable farmer. Her Dartmouth, MA-based business, Eva's Garden, has been growing organic herbs and greens for over thirty years. The area's best chefs continue to seek out and use her herbs year after year, especially if they're looking for something more exotic.

In 1965, Eva started out studying pottery at the Rhode Island School of Design in Providence but fell in love with the South Coast while visiting friends. She began spending weekends here and after, a couple of years, she and her husband George bought the property that is now home to her famous garden.

Whether it's the stem, seed, or flower, Eva can most definitely tell you what each part of a plant is good for. Eva's real specialty is with uncommon herbs and wild edibles, such as purslane and goosefoot. Now in her seventies, Eva has earned a legendary reputation for both her knowledge of edible plants and her passion for what she does.

green salad with fresh herb vinaigrette + chive blossoms

SERVES 2-4

There is always a great variety of lettuce to choose from when the farmers' markets are in full swing. For this salad, start by shopping for what's fresh and in season and let the ingredients you find inspire your own garden mix. Try a combination of different kinds of lettuces, herbs and garnishes—just about anything works here. This is my go-to vinaigrette, and it has a wonderful balance of fresh flavors. The chive blossoms provide a beautiful garnish and a subtle hint of onion.

Fresh Herb Vinaigrette
1   large shallot, roughly chopped
1   tablespoon Dijon mustard
1   cup packed fresh flat-leaf Italian parsley
2   tablespoons chopped fresh thyme
    Kosher salt, to taste
    Freshly ground black pepper, to taste
2-3 tablespoons white wine vinegar
1/2 cup plus 1-2 tablespoons extra virgin olive oil

1   large bunch fresh garden greens, washed and dried
    Small handful of chive blossoms, for garnish

1. Make vinaigrette. Place shallots, mustard, parsley, and thyme in a blender and season with salt and pepper. Add 2 tablespoons vinegar and pulse. Remove top from blender and slowly stream in 1/2 cup olive oil and purée until thick and smooth. Taste for flavor and add additional vinegar for tartness or more olive oil if dressing is too thick.
2. Place salad greens in a large bowl and toss with enough vinaigrette to lightly coat. Transfer salad to a serving bowl, top with chive blossoms, season with salt and pepper, and serve immediately.

cook's note: Use leftover blossoms in scrambled eggs, served over a bowl of pasta tossed with olive oil and lemon, or chop them up and stir into some softened goat cheese for a quick sandwich spread. Taste and use the blossoms sparingly, however, as they can be a touch bitter.

creamed summer corn

SERVES 4

While not the healthiest way to enjoy the abundance of fresh summer corn, this dish is pure comfort in a bowl. The key to this recipe is using really good corn and equally good cheese. I buy a big wedge of Parmigiano-Reggiano and pulse it in the food processor until it's finely chopped. It keeps perfectly in the refrigerator for weeks and is ready to go anytime you need it.

4   ears corn, husks and silks removed
2   tablespoons unsalted butter
    Kosher salt, to taste
    Freshly ground black pepper, to taste
2   tablespoons flour
1   cup low-sodium vegetable stock
1/2 cup heavy cream
2   tablespoons chopped fresh flat-leaf Italian parsley
1/4 cup freshly grated Parmigiano-Reggiano, plus extra for garnish

1. Remove kernels from each ear of corn. One ear at a time, cut off end of cob and stand it straight up. With a sharp paring knife, carefully cut off corn kernels from cob and place in a large bowl. (When completed, you should have approximately 3 1/2-4 cups when finished). Set kernels aside and discard cobs.
2. In a medium sauté pan, heat butter over medium-low heat. Add corn kernels and season with salt and pepper. Cook until corn is softened and starts to turn bright yellow, about 10 minutes.
3. Stir in flour and cook until it is incorporated, about 1 minute. Reduce heat to low, add stock and cream, and stir to combine. Cook until mixture thickens, about 2-3 minutes.
4. Stir in parsley and Parmigiano-Reggiano and cook until warmed through, about 1-2 minutes. Transfer to a serving bowl and top with additional Parmigiano-Reggiano. Serve immediately.

CHEF RECIPE

roasted zucchini + summer squash salad with creamy basil vinaigrette

SERVES 6

From Mark Gaier and Clark Frasier, Chef/Owners, Arrow's Restaurant, Ogunquit, ME.

Mainers have been known to throw zucchini and summer squash in strangers' cars just to get rid of their bumper crops! Okay, that could be an old wives' tale, but it gets the point across: these squash crops have a way of overwhelming even the most talented cook. This delicious preparation almost solves the problem. People love this dish; it's creamy, smoky, and delicious—the perfect summer fare. And even better, it's super easy to prepare!

1   large zucchini, cut into 1/4-inch thick rounds
1   large summer squash, cut into 1/4-inch thick rounds
6   tablespoons extra virgin olive oil, divided
     Kosher salt, to taste
     Freshly ground black pepper, to taste
1/2   Vidalia onion, thinly sliced

Creamy Basil Vinaigrette
1/2   bunch fresh basil
1/4   bunch fresh flat-leaf Italian parsley
2   tablespoons red wine vinegar
1   teaspoon Dijon mustard
1/2   cup plain yogurt
1/4   cup sour cream
1/4   cup extra virgin olive oil

1/2   head of green leaf lettuce, roughly chopped
1/2   head of red leaf lettuce, roughly chopped

1. Preheat oven to 400°F.
2. Place zucchini and summer squash in a bowl, drizzle with 3 tablespoons olive oil, and season with salt and pepper. Place vegetable rounds on a roasting pan and cook until just tender, 8-10 minutes.
3. Place onion in a bowl, drizzle with 2 tablespoons olive oil, and season with salt and pepper. Place onion slices on another roasting pan and cook until tender and slightly caramelized, 5-7 minutes.
4. Once squash and onions are done, set both aside and allow to them cool completely.
5. While cooling, place a medium-sized pot of water on stove, generously season with salt, and allow water to come to a rapid boil.
6. Make vinaigrette. Remove any stems from basil and parsley, making sure you only have leaves. Place a bowl of ice water next to pot of boiling water. Place herbs in boiling water for 45 seconds to 1 minute and quickly transfer to ice water for about 5 minutes to stop cooking process (this allows herbs to stay bright green). Transfer herbs, once completely cooled, onto a few paper towels and allow them to dry. While herbs are drying, put vinegar, mustard, yogurt, and sour cream in a blender. Purée until everything is incorporated. With blender running, add blanched herbs to blender, slowly drizzle in 1/4 cup olive oil, and season with salt and pepper (dressing should be a vibrant green color and very smooth). Place in refrigerator to keep cool. Dressing will last in the refrigerator for approximately 4-5 days before discoloring.
7. Assemble salad. In a large mixing bowl, gently toss cooked zucchini, summer squash, and onions and season with salt and pepper. Toss with remaining 1 tablespoon olive oil. Add salad greens and just enough dressing to coat everything. Toss together and divide equally among serving plates, placing a few pieces of squash and zucchini on top for garnish.

cook's note: To avoid the oven on a hot summer day, grill the zucchini and summer squash instead, which adds a nice charred flavor to the dish. To grill the onion, cut it into thick slices (so they hold together on the grill) and dice before adding to the salad. You could also thread the slices onto a skewer and grill them until lightly charred, about 5-7 minutes.

FARM FRESH RHODE ISLAND

Farm Fresh Rhode Island was founded in 2004 as a local food system that links farmers and consumers in order to build healthier communities around good, fresh food. By preserving farmland and agricultural resources, the organization has proven the ancillary benefits of eating and shopping local—job creation, economic growth, agricultural-based tourism, and improved quality of life. Of course, the best benefit of all is the increased availability to wholesome, local foods for all Rhode Islanders.

Farm Fresh Rhode Island strives to make local food more accessible to the larger community through the sponsorship of programs such as the Farm to School program; an array of year-round farmers' markets; and distribution channels that deliver locally grown products to restaurants, hospitals, schools, and food banks. With a dedicated mission to make fresh, local food the center of the dinner table, Farm Fresh Rhode Island has established itself as a vital resource in the Ocean State.

free-form garden lasagna

SERVES 4

This is a rustic interpretation of lasagna, using slices of zucchini as the "noodles," which are stacked with fresh, sautéed garden spinach and flavorful, gooey cheese. It's a bit messy, but oh so worth it. This recipe works best with large zucchini cut into thick slices so they will hold up in the dish (and the zucchini will shrink a bit after they're roasted). Fresh basil pesto and homemade tomato sauce perfectly round out the flavors, and a crusty baguette is always welcome to help gather up any remaining sauce left behind.

- 1 large, straight zucchini
- 5 tablespoons extra virgin olive oil, divided
  Kosher salt, to taste
  Freshly ground black pepper, to taste
- 1¼ cups simple year-round tomato sauce (see page 72)
- 2 cloves garlic, divided
- 1 cup packed fresh basil leaves
- ¼ cup freshly grated Parmigiano-Reggiano, plus extra for garnish
- 1 cup ricotta cheese
- 1 medium onion, thinly sliced
- 4 cups packed chopped fresh spinach leaves
- 1 buffalo mozzarella ball, cut into 8 slices

1. Preheat oven at 425°F.
2. Trim off ends of zucchini and discard. Stand zucchini up on a cutting board and cut lengthwise into 4 long, thick slices (save any remaining zucchini for another use). Cut each slice in half, making 8 pieces total. Place zucchini slices on a large baking sheet, toss with 2 tablespoons olive oil, and season with salt and pepper. Roast zucchini, turning over once halfway through cooking, until lightly golden brown, about 20-25 minutes (amount of time will vary depending on thickness of zucchini). Set aside.
3. Set oven to broil.
4. Place tomato sauce in a small saucepan and place over low heat to keep warm.
5. Make basil pesto. Roughly chop 1 clove of garlic and add to bowl of a food processor. Add basil and Parmigiano-Reggiano and season with salt and pepper. With motor running, slowly stream in 2 tablespoons olive oil until mixture is combined but still slightly thick. Transfer to a medium bowl.
6. Add pesto to ricotta and stir until well combined. Set aside.
7. Finely mince remaining 1 clove garlic and set aside.
8. In a large sauté pan over medium heat, add remaining 1 tablespoon olive oil. Add onion, cook until softened, about 5 minutes, and season with salt and pepper. Add garlic and cook for another 1-2 minutes. Add spinach and cook until just wilted, about 5 minutes. Set aside.
9. Transfer 4 pieces of zucchini to a plate and set aside. Evenly spread out remaining 4 pieces of zucchini on same baking sheet, leaving a bit of room between each one. Place equal amounts of ricotta mixture on top of zucchini slices on baking sheet. Top each with 2 slices of mozzarella, place baking sheet back in oven, and broil until cheese begins to melt, about 1-2 minutes.
10. Divide broiled zucchini stacks among 4 serving plates. Top each with equal amounts of spinach mixture. Place 1 piece of remaining zucchini on top of each, followed by equal amounts of tomato sauce. Garnish with additional Parmigiano-Reggiano and season with salt and pepper. Serve warm.

cook's note: Look for a large, straight zucchini for this recipe, which will make cutting the zucchini much easier (if it's too curved, you won't be able to cut it into thick slices).

zucchini ribbons with creamy goat cheese dressing

SERVES 4

At the height of the growing season, the farmers' markets are piled high with zucchini. In this recipe, the zucchini is sliced into thin ribbons, making for a lighter alternative to pasta in the heat of summer.

Creamy Goat Cheese Dressing

4   ounces goat cheese, at room temperature
2   tablespoons freshly grated Parmigiano-
    Reggiano
    Zest of ½ lemon
    Juice of 1 lemon
    Kosher salt, to taste
    Freshly ground black pepper, to taste

2   large, straight zucchini
2   tablespoons extra virgin olive oil

1. Make dressing. In a medium bowl, add goat cheese, Parmigiano-Reggiano, lemon zest, and juice and season with salt and pepper. Stir until well combined. Set aside.

2. Trim off ends of both zucchini and discard. Stand one zucchini up on a cutting board and cut lengthwise into long strips, about ⅛- to ¼-inch thick. Repeat with remaining zucchini.

3. Stack a few slices on top of each other and cut lengthwise into strands (zucchini should look like thick spaghetti). Repeat until all zucchini are sliced.

4. In a large non-stick pan, heat 1 tablespoon olive oil over medium heat. Add ½ of zucchini and season with salt and pepper. Cook, tossing zucchini until just al dente, about 5 minutes. Keep zucchini in a single layer so they cook evenly. Transfer zucchini to a bowl. Repeat with remaining olive oil and zucchini. When all of zucchini are cooked, return both batches to pan and warm through, about 1-2 minutes.

5. Divide zucchini among serving bowls and top with goat cheese dressing.

simple year-round tomato sauce

APPROXIMATELY 3 1/2 CUPS

In the summer, you can certainly make a home-made tomato sauce using fresh ingredients, but it can be an involved process. Here's my simple tomato sauce recipe, which works well year round and when you're pressed for time.

1   tablespoon extra virgin olive oil
1/2 small onion, diced
1   clove garlic, diced
    Kosher salt, to taste
    Freshly ground black pepper, to taste
1   28-ounce can diced tomatoes
1-2 tablespoons sugar, optional

1. In a medium saucepan, heat oil over medium heat. Add onion and cook for about 5-10 minutes, until softened. Season with salt and pepper. Add garlic and cook for another 1-2 minutes. Reduce heat and add tomatoes. Cover pan and simmer over low heat for about 30 minutes.
2. Transfer mixture to a food processor and blend until smooth. Return mixture to saucepan and keep on warm until ready to use. Add sugar to cut acidity. Store any leftover sauce in freezer for up to one month.

heirloom tomatoes with feta + olives

SERVES 4

The robust flavors of a Greek salad inspired this dish. With its salty feta and slightly tart, vinegary dressing, these beautiful slices of heirloom tomatoes don't need much else. You'll fall in love with their deep red, yellow, green, and purple hues, but it's their tender, sweet flavor that will keep you coming back for more.

4   large heirloom tomatoes, sliced about
    1/2-inch thick
    Kosher salt, to taste
    Freshly ground black pepper, to taste
1   cup crumbled feta cheese
1/3 cup black olives, chopped and pitted
2   tablespoons extra virgin olive oil
2   teaspoons red wine vinegar
1/2 teaspoon hand-torn fresh oregano

1. Place heirloom tomatoes down center of a large serving platter and season with salt and pepper. Scatter feta cheese and olives over top and set aside.
2. In a small bowl, combine olive oil, red wine vinegar, and oregano. Season with salt and pepper. Taste for seasonings and add in more vinegar (for tartness) or oil (if too tart). Drizzle over tomatoes and serve immediately.

smashed potato salad

SERVES 6-8

A few summers ago, a friend asked me to bring a potato salad to a party. And while no backyard party is complete without potato salad, it's a frequent and often overlooked side dish. I decided to play around with my old standby. I left the skins on and smashed the potatoes slightly so that the finished salad had both small and large chunks of potatoes. I tossed it all together with the dressing, and right before serving, I folded in some crumbled blue cheese. The result was a huge hit, and this salad is now one of my most-requested recipes.

8	large eggs
2	tablespoons Dijon mustard
2	tablespoons honey
1/4	cup white wine vinegar
	Kosher salt, to taste
	Freshly ground black pepper
1/2	cup extra virgin olive oil
8	medium Yukon gold potatoes (approximately 2 1/2 pounds)
4	scallions, white and light green parts, thinly sliced
2	large celery stalks, minced
1/2	cup roughly chopped celery leaves
1/2	cup roughly chopped flat-leaf parsley
4	ounces crumbled blue cheese, or to taste

1. Place eggs in a saucepan and fill with enough cold water to cover eggs by about 1 inch. Bring to a gentle boil; remove from heat. Cover and let stand for 12 minutes. Drain and rinse eggs with cold water. Allow eggs to cool to room temperature while you prepare rest of recipe.
2. In a large bowl, combine mustard, honey, and vinegar, and season with salt and pepper. Slowly whisk in 1/2 cup olive oil to emulsify. Taste for flavor and adjust if necessary (add in more honey for sweetness, more mustard for tang, or more olive oil if too thick). Set aside.
3. Meanwhile, place potatoes in a pot of cold, salted water and bring to a boil. Cook until fork tender, about 25-30 minutes. Transfer to a large bowl and set aside to cool slightly.
4. When potatoes are cool enough to handle but still warm, gently smash into large chunks using a fork. Add 1/2 of dressing to potatoes and toss, evenly coating potatoes. (Be sure to do this while potatoes are still warm so they will absorb flavor as they cool.)
5. Peel eggs and roughly chop.
6. When ready to serve, add scallions, celery, celery leaves, and parsley to potatoes and gently toss to combine. Transfer to a serving bowl and top with chopped eggs and blue cheese. Pour remaining 1/2 dressing over top and season with salt and pepper and serve.

cook's note: For this recipe, my choice is locally produced Great Hill Blue, which is available throughout the country (see page 141). To add some additional flavor to this dish, grill the scallions. Toss with olive oil and season with salt and pepper. Place on the grill and cook until lightly charred, 3-4 minutes.

chapter 4

picnic

blueberry lemonade

fresh cranberry smoothie

lemony kale hummus

yellow tomato gazpacho

chilled paella salad with shrimp

chiocciole pasta salad with yogurt dressing

lemony quinoa salad with avocado + sprouts

poached tuna, chickpeas + chopped hard-boiled egg

smoky pickled corn circles

strawberry salsa with sugared pita chips

campfire brownies

petite blueberry hand pies

The coastline of Southern New England is home to a stunning mix of quaint rural villages, farmland, salt marshes, and harbors. There is no better way to enjoy the charm of this New England landscape than to find a quiet corner and spread out a picnic blanket. These recipes make for delicious, moveable outdoor feasts, perfect for hikes, beach excursions, boat trips, or any other adventure you have planned.

blueberry lemonade

SERVES 4-6

Homemade lemonade may seem labor intensive, but the minute you start squeezing those lemons, you will be instantly transported back to your first lemonade stand. The addition of fresh blueberry juice and plump blueberries floating in your glass is a nice twist on this classic summertime drink.

2   pints (4 cups) fresh blueberries, picked through
14   lemons, divided
4   cups cold water
1/2 cup sugar
     Ice, for serving

1. Place a half pint of blueberries in a small bowl and set aside.
2. Place remaining 1 1/2 pints blueberries in a blender along with juice from 2 lemons and purée until smooth. Pour half of puréed blueberries into a fine-mesh strainer set over a large glass measuring cup and, using a spatula, gently force blueberries to release their liquid into cup. Scrape excess liquid from bottom of strainer into measuring cup. Discard blueberry pulp from strainer. Rinse strainer and repeat with remaining 1/2 of puréed blueberries (you should have about 1 1/2 cups of strained blueberry juice when finished). Rinse strainer and set aside.
3. Add juice from 6 lemons to blueberry juice in measuring cup. Stir to combine (pour through a fine mesh strainer one last time, if desired).
4. Pour mixture into a large pitcher and add juice from remaining 6 lemons. Add water and stir. Add 1/4 cup sugar and taste. Add more sugar, 1 tablespoon at a time, until you reach desired level of sweetness (amount of sugar you use will depend on your own preference and how sweet blueberries are).
5. Cover pitcher with plastic wrap and chill until ready to serve.
6. Spoon ice into 4-6 serving glasses and add a few reserved blueberries to each glass. Give pitcher of lemonade a good stir and pour over ice. Serve immediately.

cook's note: For an adult version, serve with a splash of your favorite vodka.

fresh cranberry smoothie

MAKES 2 8-OUNCE SMOOTHIES

Cranberries are a great ingredient for a smoothie, providing a bright, tart alternative to more traditional berry flavors. I buy fresh cranberries and keep them in the freezer to enjoy in smoothies all year long, but if you already have a bag of frozen cranberries, those will work too. In fact, frozen cranberries make the smoothie thicker, as do the prunes, which also work as a natural sweetener. Pour the finished smoothie into a portable cup or thermos and take it with you as you head out for the day. It's a great way to start any beach day.

1   cup ice
1   cup frozen cranberries
12   prunes, pitted
12   ounces plain Greek yogurt
3/4   cup cranberry juice, or to taste
2-3   tablespoons honey, or to taste

1. In a blender, chop ice. Add cranberries, prunes, yogurt, cranberry juice, and 2 tablespoons honey and blend until smooth. Taste for tartness and add in a bit more honey if desired. Add more cranberry juice if smoothie is too thick.

lemony kale hummus

MAKES APPROXIMATELY 1¹/₂ CUPS

This green-hued version of a traditional hummus is full of nutrients from the addition of kale. For this recipe, I use curly kale—instead of Lacinato (or Tuscan) kale—because of its slightly peppery taste. Kale hummus tastes great served on crackers or spread on a sandwich. It is best the day you make it, but will last covered in the refrigerator for up to 2 days (the longer it sits, however, the less vibrant the color will be).

¹/₂	bunch curly kale, stemmed and roughly chopped
1	15-ounce can chickpeas, drained and rinsed
¹/₄	cup freshly grated Parmigiano-Reggiano
	Zest from 1 lemon
	Juice from 1-2 lemons
1	small clove garlic, chopped
	Kosher salt, to taste
	Freshly ground black pepper, to taste
¹/₄	cup plus 1-2 tablespoons extra virgin olive oil

1. Bring a large pot of water to a boil. Add kale and blanch until bright green in color, about 5 minutes. Remove with a slotted spoon and place in a bowl of ice water for 5 minutes to shock kale and preserve bright green color.
2. Drain kale and squeeze out any excess liquid. Place in a food processor along with chickpeas, Parmigiano-Reggiano, lemon zest, juice from 1 lemon, and garlic and season with salt and pepper. Pulse until incorporated. With motor running, slowly stream in ¹/₄ cup olive oil and process until smooth, scraping down sides of bowl as necessary. Taste for seasoning and add in juice from another ¹/₂-1 lemon if desired (or more olive oil if mixture is too thick). Refrigerate until ready to serve.

yellow tomato gazpacho

SERVES 4-6

Gazpacho is one of my favorite soups to make in the summer because the longer it sits the better it gets. It's perfect for a picnic (simply transport it in individual mason jars) or as a light and refreshing meal at home. Yellow tomatoes make a mild and sweet gazpacho, and the orange juice and vinegar provide a sweet and slightly tart finish.

6	large (or 8 medium) yellow tomatoes
1	medium cucumber, peeled, seeded, and chopped
¹/₂	yellow bell pepper, cored, seeded, and chopped
¹/₂	small yellow onion, chopped
2	cloves garlic, roughly chopped
	Kosher salt, to taste
	Freshly ground black pepper, to taste
2	tablespoons champagne (or white wine) vinegar
2	tablespoons orange juice
2	tablespoons extra virgin olive oil, plus extra for garnish
	Cherry tomatoes, cut in half, for garnish

1. Bring a large pot of water to a boil. Cut a small "X" in bottom of each tomato. Place tomatoes in boiling water for 1-2 minutes. When skin starts to visibly pull away, remove tomatoes with tongs and transfer to bowl of ice water. Allow to cool for 5 minutes. Using your fingers or a paring knife, remove and discard tomato skins and cores. Chop tomatoes.
2. Add tomatoes and their juices (in batches) to a food processor and pulse until completely smooth. Transfer each batch of tomatoes to one large bowl. To food processor, add cucumber, yellow bell pepper, onion, and garlic; season with salt and pepper and pulse until completely smooth. Transfer mixture to bowl of tomatoes and stir to combine. Stir in vinegar, orange juice, and olive oil. Cover with plastic wrap and refrigerate until ready to serve, at least 2 hours or up to 2 days.
3. To serve, ladle soup into serving bowls (or mason jars), garnish with cut cherry tomatoes, followed by a drizzle of olive oil, season with salt and pepper, and serve cold.

CRANBERRY COUNTRY

Few other fruits can lay claim to as much as the cranberry. Consider the following: With over fourteen thousand acres of working cranberry bogs spread across Southeastern Massachusetts and Cape Cod, this humble little fruit is Massachusetts' number one agricultural product. It is one of only three fruits believed to be native to North America. Entire festivals are devoted to its harvest, and it just wouldn't be Thanksgiving without it.

It's not surprising, then, that this little fruit also has a long and colorful history. Long before Europeans arrived in North America, Native Americans were using cranberries for medicinal properties, as a dyeing agent, and a preservative for meat. Settlers quickly caught on and also found that the fruit was a valuable bartering tool. Whalers out of New Bedford likely carried cranberries aboard their ships in order to ward off scurvy (when it comes to antioxidants, cranberries outrank nearly every superfood).

Cranberries are harvested in the fall when the berries are deep red in color. During the harvest, from September through early November, there are an abundance of regional fairs and festivals where visitors can experience the workings of a cranberry bog first hand. Many of these festivals include tours and tastings, as well as rides into a bog. Given that cranberry cultivation is such an important part of the regional economy, these festivals often take on an air of community celebration.

Cranberry bogs were made by glacial deposits thousands of years ago, and as distinctive as these ecosystems are, they are actually rather harsh; luckily, cranberries are resilient plants. The fruit grows on vines firmly rooted in beds of sand, peat, gravel, and clay. Some vines in Massachusetts are estimated to be more than 150 years old.

Such a special fruit requires a unique method of harvesting. Today, methods depend upon the end use of the berries. The fresh berries found in the produce aisle are typically "dry harvested." The fruit is separated from their vines with machines that look a little like upright lawn mowers. The berries are eventually removed by helicopters to avoid damaging the bog.

The cranberries used in juices, sauces, or other products are "wet harvested." The bog is flooded and machines are used to agitate the water, dislodging the fruit from the vines. As cranberries have little pockets of air inside them, they float. Farmers use this to their advantage, corralling them into large nets before trucking them off to the receiving plant.

Some area cranberry growers have also been at the forefront of sustainable farming practices. Carver-based Edgewood Bogs, in particular is a standout. The fourth-generation family business has worked hard in recent years to reduce their carbon footprint, building a sustainable processing facility powered by solar energy and working to conserve resources and reduce waste whenever possible.

How can you tell a good berry from a bad one? Bounce it. A good cranberry has a vibrant red color, is firm, and bounces with ease.

chilled paella salad with shrimp

SERVES 4

This delicious salad has all the same flavors of traditional Spanish paella, but is far easier to enjoy on a picnic. Small garden cherry tomatoes add a lovely burst of color when tossed with the saffron rice. I find it is best to make the salad ahead of time and keep it chilled until you're ready to pack it up.

1	tablespoon extra virgin olive oil
1/2	small onion, finely minced
	Kosher salt, to taste
	Freshly ground black pepper, to taste
1	large clove garlic, finely minced
2	cups water
1/4	teaspoon saffron
1	cup long grain white rice
1	pound extra large shrimp, washed, peeled, and deveined
2	lemons, divided
1	bay leaf
1	pint cherry tomatoes, cut in half
1/4	cup roughly chopped fresh flat-leaf Italian parsley, for garnish

1. In a small sauté pan, heat olive oil over medium heat. Add onion and cook until softened, about 5 minutes. Season with salt and pepper. Add garlic and cook for another 1-2 minutes. Set aside to cool.
2. In a medium saucepan, add water and crumble in saffron, gently crushing it with your fingers. Bring water to a boil, add rice, reduce heat to low, and cover. Cook until rice is tender and water has evaporated, about 15 minutes. Remove from heat and allow rice to cool to room temperature.
3. Pat dry shrimp and set aside.
4. Cut 1 lemon in half. Cut other lemon into wedges. Transfer lemon wedges to a small serving dish and set aside.
5. Add lemon halves to a large saucepan, along with bay leaf, a pinch of salt, and about 4 cups of water. Bring to a boil. Lower heat to medium and add shrimp. Cook until shrimp turn bright pink and are cooked through, about 2-3 minutes.
6. Drain and transfer shrimp to a bowl of ice water. Cool for about 2-3 minutes. Remove shrimp, pat dry, and set aside.
7. When everything is cooled to room temperature, place rice in a large bowl. Add cooled onion mixture and stir to combine. Add shrimp and cherry tomatoes to bowl, but do not stir them in. Cover with plastic wrap and chill for about 1 hour.
8. When ready to serve, gently stir in shrimp and cherry tomatoes. Garnish with parsley and serve with lemon wedges for drizzling.

chiocciole pasta salad
with yogurt dressing

SERVES 6

A good, old-fashioned barbecue requires a
pasta salad, but standard recipes often fall short.
A few updates take it to a whole new level, like
using chiocciole pasta, which means "snail"
in Italian. Not only are these noodles slightly bigger,
but they also have more crevices, making them
perfect for hiding pockets of the thick, creamy
dressing. Replacing some of the mayonnaise with
yogurt makes this dressing lighter, and the lemon
juice and Dijon mustard give it plenty of tang. Enjoy
this salad the day it's made, after it's had some time
to chill in the refrigerator.

1   pound chiocciole pasta
1/2 red onion, minced
1   large celery stalk, minced
1/2 cup celery leaves, minced
1/4 cup finely minced fresh flat-leaf Italian parsley
6   ounces plain Greek yogurt
1/2 cup plus 2 tablespoons mayonnaise
     Juice from 1 lemon
1   tablespoon Dijon mustard
     Kosher salt, to taste
     Freshly ground black pepper, to taste

1. Bring a large pot of salted water to a boil. Add
   pasta and cook until al dente, about 7-10 minutes.
   Drain and rinse pasta under cold water. Allow to
   cool completely to room temperature, stirring every
   so often to prevent it from sticking.
2. Transfer cooled pasta to a large bowl. Add red
   onion, celery, celery leaves, and parsley to bowl.
3. In a medium bowl, combine yogurt, mayonnaise,
   lemon juice, and mustard until smooth and season
   with salt and pepper. Add dressing to bowl of pasta
   and toss together, coating pasta and vegetables.
   Cover with plastic wrap and allow salad to chill in
   refrigerator for about 30 minutes before serving.

cook's note: Chiocciole pasta is fairly easy to find
these days, but if you can't locate it, regular elbow
or rigatoni will work. Look for pasta that has some
ridges, crevices, and hollows that will hold the
dressing.

lemony quinoa salad
with avocado + sprouts

SERVES 4

Quinoa is a hearty grain packed with protein
and makes a great salad with some depth to it.
Here it's infused with lemon flavor and served with
avocados and wisps of alfalfa sprouts scattered
over the top. It's great as is, topped with feta or
goat cheese, or served with my backyard bbq
chicken (see page 130).

2   cups quinoa, rinsed
4   cups water
2   tablespoons extra virgin olive oil, plus
     extra for drizzling
     Zest and juice from 2 lemons, divided
     Kosher salt, to taste
     Freshly ground black pepper
2   Hass avocados
     Alfalfa sprouts
1/2 cup roughly chopped fresh flat-leaf Italian
     parsley

1. In a medium saucepan, bring quinoa and water
   to a boil. Reduce heat to low and place a cover
   on top of pot, slightly ajar, for about 2 minutes, until
   water settles down (so it doesn't overflow). Once
   it settles, cover completely and simmer until grains
   are translucent and germ ring is visible, about
   10-15 minutes. Transfer to a large bowl and toss
   with olive oil and zest from both lemons and juice
   from 1 lemon. Season with salt and pepper and
   set aside.
2. Halve avocados, remove pits, and scoop out
   flesh. Place avocados on a cutting board, cut side
   down, and cut into slices. Drizzle with juice from
   1/2 lemon.
3. Transfer quinoa to a large serving platter. Place
   avocado slices down center of platter and top
   with some alfalfa sprouts, just enough to lightly
   cover top of platter (or more to taste if desired).
   Scatter parsley over top and drizzle platter with
   juice from remaining 1/2 lemon and some additional
   olive oil. Season with salt and pepper and serve
   immediately.

poached tuna, chickpeas + chopped hard-boiled egg

SERVES 4

A salad from the Shipyard Galley in Mattapoisett, MA inspired this dish. Here, fresh tuna is poached and tossed with a tart dressing, chickpeas, and diced red onion. I prefer equal parts vinegar and olive oil in the dressing but you can adjust this ratio to your preference. I pack this salad in jars (such as weck or mason jars) for a casual—yet delicious—lunch on the beach.

1	pound fresh tuna
4	extra large eggs
1/4	cup extra virgin olive oil
1/4	cup red wine vinegar
	Kosher salt, to taste
	Freshly ground black pepper, to taste
1	15-ounce can chickpeas, drained and rinsed
1/2	cup roughly chopped fresh flat-leaf Italian parsley
1/4	red onion, diced

1. Place tuna in a large saucepan and fill with enough water to cover tuna by about 1 inch. Bring to a gentle simmer (do not boil) until fish is cooked through and easily flakes apart, about 10-12 minutes. Remove from water (avoiding any skim that might have formed on top), transfer to a bowl, and allow to cool.
2. Place eggs in a saucepan and fill with enough cold water to cover eggs by about 1 inch. Bring to a gentle boil; remove from heat. Cover and let stand for 12 minutes. Drain and rinse eggs with cold water. Let stand for 5 minutes, and then peel off shells. Roughly chop and set aside.
3. In a small bowl, combine oil and vinegar; season with salt and pepper and set aside.
4. When tuna is cool enough to handle, flake into bite-size pieces and place in a large bowl. Add chickpeas, parsley, and red onion and toss with about 1/2 of dressing. Transfer to a large serving platter. (If packing for a picnic, gently stir in eggs and transfer to mason jars.)
5. Scatter eggs over top of salad on platter. Pour remaining dressing over top and season with salt and pepper. Serve at room temperature.

CHEF RECIPE

smoky pickled corn circles

SERVES 6-8

From Marc DeRego, Grill Master, Smoke & Pickles, Westport, MA.

Corn circles are a great way to enjoy one of summer's most bountiful crops. In this recipe, corn cobs are cut into rounds and pickled for 3 days in a brine of sweet pineapple juice and smoky chipotle peppers, giving the finished corn a wonderful contrast of flavors. Corn circles are a delicious (and unexpected) side dish for a picnic or barbecue.

6   ears sweet corn, husks and silks removed
6   tomatillos
2   teaspoons vegetable oil
2   large onions, cut into thin rings
2   red peppers, cut into medium julienned strips
8   cloves garlic
4   cups white wine vinegar
2   cups water
1½ cups sugar
1   cup pineapple juice
2   tablespoons kosher salt
1   tablespoon plus 1 teaspoon Dijon mustard
1   tablespoon whole cloves
6   chipotle peppers in adobo sauce
3   tablespoons fresh cilantro berries

1. Bring a large pot of water to a boil. Add corn and blanch until kernels plump, about 3 minutes. Remove and set aside to cool.
2. Remove papery outer layer from tomatillos, rinse tomatillos under warm water, and cut each in half.
3. Place a large sauté pan over low heat and add oil. Add tomatillos, onion, peppers, and garlic, sweat until vegetables are slightly softened, about 15 minutes, and set aside to cool.
4. When corn has cooled, cut each ear into 6 equal pieces and set aside.
5. In a large, non-reactive pot, combine white wine vinegar, water, sugar, pineapple juice, salt, mustard, and cloves and bring to a rolling boil. Add chipotles and remove from heat. Allow brine to cool to room temperature.
6. When brine has cooled, add fresh cilantro berries, corn, and cooled vegetables and stir. Store, covered in refrigerator, for at least 3 days (and up to 3 weeks).

cook's note: I grow cilantro, pick the berries early in the summer, and then freeze them to use throughout the season. You can often find cilantro berries through local growers or at specialty food stores as well.

SMOKE AND PICKLES

Smoke and Pickles is a somewhat whimsical culinary collaboration between renowned pickle master Dan George (co-author of *Quick Pickles: Easy Recipes with Big Flavor* with Chris Schlesinger and John Willoughby), Sally Huntington, Marc DeRego, Kristen Rogers, and Chris Ash. Each Smoke and Pickle member brings his or her own experience from the food world, and they pretty much have all the bases covered, from foraging and event planning, to pickling, cooking, and fiddling. This cumulative wisdom and undeniable panache for innovative and delicious fare have blended together harmoniously. The result is a unique catering company with a mission to serve up the very best of what the South Coast has to offer.

It all begins with the wood fire, which the team brings to the event site to roast, grill, BBQ, or smoke a homespun, backyard feast for outdoor parties—from weddings to simple summer gatherings. (In fact, Dan George is known in these parts for the billowing smoker he hauls behind his car.) Menus aren't merely tailored to each client; they are artfully designed for them. Depending on the occasion and what's fresh and in season, the Smoke and Pickles team handpicks ingredients from local farms and fishing boats in order to craft a meal that will stop guests in their tracks. The menu is paired with any of thirty different kinds of pickles, relishes, and salsas that Smoke and Pickles offers.

This distinctive catering experience is perfect for foodies who want something out of the ordinary to mark special occasions in a truly memorable fashion.

FARMCOAST

Until recently, people may not have known we had a "FarmCoast" in Southern New England. In actual fact, it's a relatively new identity for a long-overlooked corner of the coastline that encompasses villages in both Massachusetts and Rhode Island. Even for many Bostonians, the cohesive area that is home to the picturesque towns of Tiverton, Little Compton, Westport, and Dartmouth is relatively unknown. Though divided by two states, these towns and the villages share a distinct rural charm, with farmland stretching across peninsulas bordered by salt marshes. This unique region reflects the pastoral quality of 19th century New England, preserved for visitors and residents to enjoy today.

It's not surprising that these towns have come together to craft their own identity that may help people realize the immense history and natural resources found here. There is a wealth of things to see and do along the FarmCoast, and breathtaking views and historic treasures will greet you at every turn. Whether it's a trip to Horseneck Beach in Westport, a visit to local cheese shops, a tour of a winery, or an afternoon spent antiquing, these charming towns have taken care to preserve their heritage while creating a thriving community centered around good food, the arts, and history—all of which make the FarmCoast worth a visit.

strawberry salsa with sugared pita chips

SERVES 4-6

This salsa of fresh summer strawberries is a showstopper, especially when paired with these sweet pita chips dusted with cinnamon and sugar. As with any salsa, you can adjust the desired level of spice to your own liking by adding in more jalapeño or even leaving in some of the seeds (where the real spice is). This salsa is best made right before you serve it, but if you need to make it ahead of time, just drain any excess liquid from the bottom of the bowl (the fresher the strawberries, the more liquid will accumulate).

Sugared Pita Chips
2   tablespoons unsalted butter
2   pitas
1   teaspoon sugar
1/8   teaspoon ground cinnamon

Strawberry Salsa
1   pint strawberries, washed, hulled, and diced
1/4   small white onion, finely minced
1/2   jalapeño pepper, seeded and finely minced
1   tablespoon finely minced fresh mint (or cilantro)
    Kosher salt, to taste
    Juice from 1/2-1 lime

1. Preheat oven to 425°F.
2. Make sugared pita chips. In a small saucepan, melt butter.
3. In a small bowl, combine sugar and cinnamon.
4. Using a sharp knife, gently split open edges of each pita at its seam, separating each into two rounds. Using a pastry brush, gently brush melted butter on coarse inner side of each round. Sprinkle tops with a little bit of cinnamon sugar. Repeat with remaining pita rounds. Cut each round into desired shapes. Spread pitas out in a single layer onto 1-2 baking sheets. Bake until golden brown, about 3-4 minutes. Set aside to cool.
5. Make salsa. In a medium bowl, add strawberries, onion, jalapeño, mint (or cilantro), a pinch of salt, and lime juice from 1/2 lime and gently toss together until combined. Adjust seasonings, adding in more lime juice if necessary. Transfer to a serving bowl and serve with chips.

cook's note: Any store-bought pita bread will work for this recipe, but when I want to get it fresh, I head to Sam's Bakery in Fall River, MA. This small, family-run bakery is producing some of the most delicious homemade pita around. Walk in early in the morning and you'll find warm pita bread being made right in the back of the shop—if you're lucky enough to get them while they're still hot, all the better. Make sure to grab a meat pie (or a dozen!) on your way out. Made with a special blend of meat and spices and wrapped in a pillow of homemade dough, these little concoctions are pure heaven. Chances are you'll have eaten one before you even leave the parking lot. You won't be alone—everyone does!

campfire brownies

MAKES 9 SQUARE BROWNIES

The culmination of any good outdoor party has to be roasting marshmallows around a bonfire. A gooey, slightly charred marshmallow sandwiched between chocolate and graham crackers is a timeless combination that will remind you of your childhood. This recipe is based on all of those classic flavors, but it is a much more manageable version, perfect for parties, picnics, or off-season cravings—no fire pit required!

Crust

Cooking spray
6 tablespoons unsalted butter
1 1/3 cups graham cracker crumbs, finely ground
2 tablespoons sugar
Pinch kosher salt

Brownies

1 1/2 sticks unsalted butter, cut into pieces
6 ounces semisweet chocolate, roughly chopped
1 1/4 cups plus 1 tablespoon sugar
3 large eggs, at room temperature
1 1/2 teaspoons vanilla extract
3/4 cup flour
1/2 teaspoon kosher salt

12 large marshmallows

1. Preheat oven to 350°F.
2. Line an 8 x 8-inch baking pan with parchment paper, making sure that two sides hang over edges by about 1 inch (this will allow you to easily pull brownies out of pan). Coat parchment paper and all sides of pan with cooking spray and set aside.
3. Make crust. In a small saucepan, melt butter. In a medium bowl, combine graham cracker crumbs, sugar, and salt. Add melted butter and mix well. Press crumb mixture evenly over bottom of prepared pan with a spatula and bake until just golden brown around edges of pan, about 10 minutes.
4. Meanwhile, make brownie batter. Place a medium glass bowl over a medium saucepan filled with about 1-2 inches of water (make sure water doesn't touch bottom of glass bowl). Add butter and chocolate to glass bowl and melt over very low heat, stirring occasionally as chocolate melts. When mixture is melted, remove from heat and transfer mixture to a large bowl. Allow to cool for 5 minutes. Add sugar and stir to combine with melted chocolate. Slowly whisk in eggs a bit at a time (if chocolate is too hot it will scramble eggs). Add vanilla and stir until incorporated. Slowly add in flour in 2 batches and stir until just incorporated. Stir in salt. Do not over mix.
5. Pour batter over graham crackers and bake until brownies are set and center is still a bit soft (see cook's note), about 25-30 minutes.
6. Remove pan from oven, move oven rack to top position, and turn on broiler. Place marshmallows evenly over top of brownies and place pan in oven. Broil until marshmallows are softened and lightly toasted, about 45 seconds to 1 minute. Carefully pull pan out from oven and, using back of a tablespoon, gently press down on marshmallows to flatten slightly (do this slowly so that they don't stick to your spoon). Return pan to oven and broil until marshmallows are toasted, another 15-30 seconds. Remove pan and allow brownies to cool for at least 1 hour, allowing them to fully set. Gently lift parchment paper out of pan (you may have to run a knife along outside edges of pan as marshmallows are very sticky!). Transfer brownies to a cutting board.
7. Run a sharp knife under warm water and cut brownies into squares, ensuring each has some marshmallow on top. (After each cut, run knife back under warm water, wipe clean, and repeat this process until all of brownies are cut.)

cook's note: Be sure not to over-bake the brownies. They should be soft but still a bit gooey when tested with a toothpick (you want moist crumbles on the toothpick when they are done). Start checking them after 15 minutes and every few minutes thereafter.

petite blueberry hand pies

MAKES 16-18 PIES

Hand pies (or turnovers) are perfect for summertime excursions because they're easy to eat when you're on the go. I recommend using a 3-inch cookie cutter, which results in a dainty treat, but you can cut them into whatever size you prefer. Make sure the blueberries are well mashed as it will be far easier to fill the rounds. But, no matter how hard you try to keep the filling enclosed in the dough, some of it will ooze out while they bake. Don't worry—it gives them even more rustic charm.

Filling

1/2 pint (1 cup) blueberries, washed, dried, and picked over
2-3 tablespoons sugar (see cook's note)
2 teaspoons cornstarch
Zest from 1/2 lemon

Crust

2 cups flour, plus extra for dusting
1 tablespoon sugar
1 teaspoon salt
1 stick unsalted butter, cut into 8 pieces and chilled
6 tablespoons (or more) ice water
1 egg, beaten
2-4 teaspoons turbinado sugar, for sprinkling

1. Make filling. In a medium saucepan, add blueberries, sugar, cornstarch, and lemon zest. Place pan over medium heat and cook for about 5-10 minutes, stirring with a heat-proof spatula to prevent blueberries from sticking. While mixture cooks, gently mash blueberries with your spatula, allowing them to release their juices. Reduce heat to low to keep mixture from bubbling and getting too hot. Once mixture has thickened, transfer to a bowl and allow it to cool to room temperature. Place bowl in refrigerator and chill until cold, about 1 hour.
2. Make crust. In a food processor, combine flour, sugar, and salt. Add butter and process until coarse crumbs form, about 10 seconds. With machine running, slowly add 1/4 cup ice water in a steady stream through feed tube. Pulse until dough holds together, no more than 10 seconds. If still crumbly,

add more ice water, 1 tablespoon at a time. Dough should not be wet or sticky. Test finished dough by squeezing a small amount together to see if it holds its shape.
3. Wrap dough in plastic and refrigerate for about 1 hour.
4. Preheat oven to 425°F.
5. Line a baking sheet with parchment paper and set aside.
6. Remove blueberries from refrigerator and set aside.
7. Lightly flour work surface, rolling pin, and hands. Make a small, thin pile of flour off to one side for dipping cookie cutter in as you cut out circles. Roll out dough into a large rectangle, about 1/8-inch thick, keeping enough flour under it to keep it from sticking. (Dust dough with flour if it begins to stick.) Dip a 3-inch cookie cutter in flour and cut out rounds. Roll out excess dough and continue cutting out rounds until all of dough is used.
8. Using a teaspoon, place a small amount of filling in center of one round. Loosely fold top of dough over filling to enclose, forming a half moon, without sealing it completely. If it closes easily, encasing all of filling, you know how much filling to use for remaining rounds (use this as your guide for remaining rounds).
9. Once filling has been placed in center of each round, lightly brush outside edge with egg. Fold top of rounds over filling to enclose, forming half moons. Gently press edges together with your fingers to seal. Using a fork, crimp sealed edges, taking care not to pierce completely through dough (dough should be tightly sealed). Brush top of each with egg and sprinkle with sugar.
10. Transfer pies to prepared baking sheet. Bake until golden brown, about 12-14 minutes. Transfer to a wire rack to cool slightly before serving. Hand pies can be stored in an airtight container at room temperature up to 3 days.

cook's note: If your blueberries are fresh, in season, and sweet, use only 2 tablespoons of sugar in the filling, otherwise use all 3 tablespoons.

chilled saketini

cocktail hour

chilled saketini

white wine sangria

beach plum mojito

corn fritters with chipotle aioli

crab cakes with old bay aioli

chouriço in puff pastry

baked brie with honey + almonds

tuna tartare with sesame

basic crostini:

    ricotta + local honey

    fresh mozzarella + roasted garlicky tomatoes

    fresh pea purée, prosciutto + parmesan

crostini with wilted kale + goat cheese

chouriço-stuffed mushrooms

shrimp toasts with scallions, ginger + sesame

modern clams casino with oregano mojo

There's no doubt about it: the best way
to end a leisurely day at the beach or on the water
is with a casual gathering of friends in the backyard,
drinks in hand. This chapter offers some refreshing
cocktails to set the mood, along with plenty of options
for nibbling.

chilled saketini

SERVES 4

Japanese cucumbers, which are less seedy than regular cucumbers, make a beautiful garnish for this sophisticated cocktail and give it a subtle hint of crispness as well.

Japanese cucumber, for garnish
Chopped ice, for serving
6   ounces vodka
6   ounces dry sake

1. Place martini glasses in freezer.
2. Cut cucumber into thin rounds and set aside.
3. Fill a cocktail shaker with ice. Add 1¹/₂ ounces vodka and 1¹/₂ ounces sake and shake well.
4. Remove martini glasses from freezer and strain mixture into chilled martini glasses. Repeat 3 more times.
5. Add a slice of cucumber to each glass and serve cold.

white wine sangria

SERVES 4-6

Vinho Verde, which translates to "green wine" in Portuguese, is so named because this wine is best served young. It's a crisp, slightly fizzy wine with subtle floral undertones that make it a perfect choice for summertime sangria. If you can't find Vinho Verde, any similar wine will do.

1   bottle Vinho Verde
¹/₂   cup Grand Marnier
¹/₄   cup sugar
1   orange, washed, dried, and cut into
        ¹/₄ inch-thick slices
1   lemon, washed, dried, and cut into
        ¹/₄ inch-thick slices
1¹/₂ cups seedless green grapes, washed,
        dried, and sliced in half
        Ice, for serving

1. In a large pitcher, add wine, Grand Marnier, and sugar and stir together. Add fruit and mix well. Chill sangria in refrigerator for 1 to 4 hours.
2. When ready to serve, remove sangria from refrigerator and stir. Add ice to each serving glass and pour in sangria, making sure to ladle in some fruit as well. Serve immediately.

cook's note: Be sure to add ice to glasses just before serving; if you add ice to the pitcher of sangria, the ice will melt and water it down.

CHEF RECIPE

beach plum mojito

SERVES 1

From Catherine Walthers, chef and cookbook author of *Raising the Salad Bar* and *Soups + Side*s, Martha's Vineyard, MA.

The beach plum bush grows on coastal plains and dunes throughout New England. Around Labor Day you can find dozens of small plums about the size of large marbles dangling from its branches. Like its commercial cousin, these wild plums have a bluish purple skin, a single pit, and a reddish, tart, tangy flesh and make unbeatable margaritas, cordials, and mojitos.

3	tablespoons beach plum juice
3	sprigs fresh mint, plus one for garnish
1	lime, rind removed and cut in half
3	tablespoons fresh squeezed orange juice
2	ounces simple syrup
2	ounces rum (Boston's own Bully Boy white rum recommended)
	Splash of club soda

1. Make beach plum juice. Place any amount of collected beach plums (stems removed and rinsed) in a saucepan. Crush slightly with a pestle or potato masher to help release their juices. Add just enough water to barely show through fruit. Bring to a boil, then simmer on medium-low for 10 minutes. Cool slightly.
2. Pour into a colander lined with a double layer of cheesecloth over a bowl to catch juice. Refrigerate until ready to serve.
3. In a tall glass, add mint sprigs and lime and gently mash with a muddler. Add 3 tablespoons beach plum juice to glass, followed by 3 tablespoons orange juice and 2 ounces simple syrup. Fill glass with ice, add 2 ounces rum, and top with club soda. Mix well with a long spoon, garnish with a sprig of mint, and serve.

cook's note: To make simple syrup, add equal parts sugar and water in a small saucepan and bring to a simmer. Stir until sugar dissolves. Remove from heat, cool to room temperature, and refrigerate until ready to use.

corn fritters with chipotle aioli

MAKES APPROXIMATELY 18-20 FRITTERS

These particular fritters are inspired by a popular appetizer served at the Boat House in Tiverton, RI. When I deep-fry something, it typically involves my neighbors, with all of us huddled around their Fry Daddy. The Fry Daddy is a handy gadget that makes deep frying super easy, but if you (or your neighbors) don't have one, this recipe works just as well in a large, deep pot. (You'll still need to make them with friends; it's far more fun, and you'll need help eating these fritters.) Regardless of the pot you use, always take caution when deep-frying. When the oil gets hot, it can splatter easily, so keep a good watch.

Chipotle Aioli

12	ounces plain Greek yogurt
2	tablespoons chipotle salsa (see cook's note), or to taste
	Kosher salt, to taste
	Freshly ground black pepper, to taste

2	medium ears corn, husks and silks removed
2	tablespoons unsalted butter
2	cups flour
1/4	cup sugar
2	tablespoons yellow cornmeal
1	tablespoon baking powder
1/4	teaspoon kosher salt
2	large eggs
1	cup milk

Vegetable oil, for frying

1. Make aioli. In a medium bowl, combine yogurt and chipotle salsa and season with salt and pepper. Stir well. Adjust level of spice as desired by adding in more chipotle salsa to taste. Transfer to a serving bowl, cover with plastic wrap, and chill until ready to serve.
2. Remove kernels from each ear of corn. One ear at a time, cut off end of cob and stand it straight up. With a sharp paring knife, carefully cut off corn kernels from cob and place in a small bowl (you'll need about 1 cup of kernels).
3. In a small saucepan, add butter over low heat and cook until completely melted. Set aside to cool.
4. In a medium bowl, combine flour, sugar, cornmeal, baking powder, and salt.
5. In another medium bowl, combine eggs, milk, and cooled butter. Fold into dry ingredients and mix until just combined. Stir in corn.
6. Line a plate with paper towels and set aside.
7. Remove chipotle aioli from refrigerator and set aside.
8. Add enough oil to a large Dutch oven or stockpot (or Fry Daddy) to come up about 2 inches on side of pan and place over medium-high heat. Test oil by dropping a small amount of batter into pot; if it bubbles, oil is ready. With a tablespoon, scoop about 1/2 tablespoon of batter and carefully drop batter into oil. (Do one as a test to see how long it takes to cook.) Fry fritters until they puff up, float to top, and are golden brown on all sides, about 5 minutes, depending on size. Continue with remaining batter, frying in batches to avoid over-crowding pot. Remove fritters with a slotted spoon and transfer to plate lined with paper towels to drain. Allow fritters to cool slightly and season with salt and pepper while still warm. Repeat with remaining fritters.
9. Serve fritters with chipotle aioli.

cook's note: This batter is exceedingly versatile and you can add just about anything to it—such as lobster, which is what the Boat House uses—or swap out the corn for minced clams instead.

You can find chipotle chiles in many gourmet markets. The small cans come in two varieties: chipotle chiles in adobo sauce and chipotle salsa. In adobo sauce, the heat comes from the actual chiles, so be sure to adjust the amount you use based on how spicy you want it to be. Chipotle salsa has all the same smoky flavor, but comes already puréed.

SID WAINER & SON

Sid Wainer & Son, located on Purchase Street in New Bedford, MA, is a gourmet outlet that has become a mecca for food lovers everywhere. What began as a modest horse-drawn produce wagon back in 1914 has become a leader in the produce and specialty foods industry.

As a child, Henry Wainer rode on the back of his father's truck, selling fruits and vegetables, visiting local farmers along the South Coast. Over the years, the number of the Wainers' visits steadily increased, their relationships with these partners became stronger, and they began to deliver fresh fruits and vegetables to their customers the same day the crops were harvested.

Times may have changed, but the Wainer philosophy has not. Today, this third-generation family company, whose busy commercial operation now ships specialty products daily to over twenty thousand restaurants across the country, maintains those relationships with local famers and artisanal food producers that helped to secure their success. Sid Wainer & Son remains committed to promoting sustainable agriculture, preserving open farmland, and bringing fresh, handpicked, high quality produce to the marketplace.

Head into the Wainer retail outlet and you are certain to find culinary inspiration. The store is packed with imported and local products. Their large selection of olive oils, vinegars, jams and preserves, patés, charcuterie, and hard-to-find ingredients (not to mention the refrigerated cheese and produce rooms) makes Sid Wainer & Son an authentic foodie paradise.

On Saturdays, the store offers another experience altogether. Their team of in-house chefs inspires and educates shoppers with dishes created from "the store's amazing selection of ingredients. Visiting the store gives you the opportunity to speak to the chefs about what they're making and to taste ingredients before you take them home.

crab cakes with old bay aioli

MAKES 4 CRAB CAKES

Crab cakes are a staple on menus and in house-holds up and down the East Coast, and most people have a preference for how they like them prepared. For me, a good crab cake starts with the crabmeat. I use a high quality lump crabmeat, which gives the crab cakes a lot more body and texture. Mixing in fresh breadcrumbs and using egg whites as a binding agent keep the cakes light. The most important thing is not to overwork the cakes when you form them. (If you fuss over them too much you'll end up with something the consistency of hockey pucks.) You can adapt this recipe for smaller, bite-size appetizers (roughly 16 crab cakes). Large or small, serve with a small dollop of aioli and some fresh microgreens as a garnish.

Old Bay Aioli

1	large egg yolk
	Juice from 1 lemon, divided
	Kosher salt, to taste
	Freshly ground black pepper, to taste
1/4	cup plus 3 tablespoons extra virgin olive oil, divided
1/4	teaspoon Old Bay Seasoning

1/2	cup (about 2 slices) chopped plain white bread, crusts removed
8	ounces lump crabmeat
2	tablespoons roughly chopped fresh flat-leaf Italian parsley
2	tablespoons mayonnaise
1	tablespoon plus 1 teaspoon Dijon mustard
1 1/2	teaspoons Old Bay Seasoning
1	large egg white
	Mixed greens, for serving

1. Make aioli. In a medium bowl, add egg yolk and juice from 1/2 lemon, season with a pinch of salt and pepper, and whisk together to combine. Slowly stream in 1/4 cup olive oil until fully incorporated, whisking mixture until it comes together and is thick (aim for a consistency of thin ketchup). Stir in a pinch of Old Bay Seasoning. Taste for seasoning and add more Old Bay if desired. Transfer to a serving bowl, cover with plastic wrap, and place in refrigerator for about 1 hour to chill (mixture will thicken even more as it chills).

2. Place bread in bowl of a food processor and pulse until finely ground (or chop finely by hand). Set aside.

3. Squeeze out any excess moisture from crabmeat. (If you are using frozen crabmeat, be sure to re-move excess water; thawed crabmeat will have a good deal of moisture in it.)

4. In a medium bowl, add drained crabmeat, parsley, mayonnaise, mustard, Old Bay Seasoning, and egg white and season with salt and pepper. Gently fold in breadcrumbs (mixture should hold together as a ball).

5. Form into 4 cakes of equal size. Transfer cakes to a clean plate, cover with plastic wrap, and refriger-ate for about 1 hour.

6. In a large non-stick pan, heat 2 tablespoons oil over medium heat. Gently fry crab cakes until nicely golden brown on bottom, about 4-5 minutes. Flip crab cakes over, loosely cover pan with lid or a piece of aluminum foil, and cook until golden brown, about another 4-5 minutes.

7. In a medium bowl, combine mixed greens with remaining juice from 1/2 lemon and remaining 1 tablespoon olive oil and season with salt and pepper.

8. Divide crab cakes among serving plates and top each with some mixed greens. Serve warm with Old Bay aioli.

cook's note: Lump crabmeat can be harder to find; I have the best luck when I shop at my local sea-food market. Old Bay is a fairly strong spice, so a little goes a long way. I start with a pinch, adding more only if I feel like it is needed. Use enough Old Bay to impart the flavor, but not so much that it overwhelms the creaminess of the aioli.

chouriço in puff pastry

MAKES 16 HORS D'OEUVRES

When chouriço is finely ground and wrapped in buttery puff pastry, these little appetizers just melt in your mouth. You can adjust the level of spice in the aioli, but don't skip it: the spicy peppers highlight the flavor of the chouriço and the aioli is a wonderful complement to this robust appetizer.

1   mild, large chouriço link, casing removed
1   small Yukon gold potato, peeled and diced
1   tablespoon extra virgin olive oil
2   tablespoons finely chopped onion
    Kosher salt, to taste
    Freshly ground black pepper, to taste
1   clove garlic, finely minced
2   tablespoons finely minced fresh flat-leaf
    Italian parsley
    Cooking spray
7-8 ounces puff pastry (1/2 of one package),
    thawed in refrigerator
    Flour, for dusting
1   egg, beaten

Hot Pepper Aioli
1/2 cup mayonnaise
1   tablespoon hot crushed peppers (see
     cook's note)

1. Cut chouriço into 1-inch pieces and place in a food processor. Pulse until finely chopped (about 2 cups when finished). Transfer to a bowl and set aside.
2. Place potatoes in a medium saucepan and add enough cold water to cover potatoes. Add a pinch of salt and bring to a boil; reduce heat to simmer until fork tender, about 15-20 minutes. Drain potatoes. Return potatoes to saucepan and smash until potatoes are mostly smooth. Transfer 1/4 cup of potatoes to bowl of chouriço.
3. In a small sauté pan, heat olive oil over medium heat. Add onions, cook until softened, about 5 minutes, and season with salt and pepper. Add garlic and cook for another 1-2 minutes. Allow to cool. Add onion and garlic mixture to chouriço and potatoes and mix to combine. Add parsley and mix until well combined (mixture should hold together when pressed between two fingers).
4. Coat a baking sheet with cooking spray and set aside.
5. Divide chouriço mixture into two equal portions. Carefully form each portion into a long roll, 8 inches long by 1 inch in diameter, using your hands to gently squeeze it into shape (mixture is fragile so do this slowly and be patient). Set aside.
6. Remove thawed puff pastry from refrigerator and place on a lightly floured work surface, with long side parallel to edge of your workspace. Cut lengthwise into 2 pieces. Roll out each piece into a rectangle about 9 inches wide and 7 inches long.
7. Using a pastry brush, lightly brush entire surface of each piece of pastry with water. Take one roll of chouriço and place it lengthwise on pastry at side nearest you, leaving about a 1/2-inch border on left and right.
8. Carefully roll chouriço in puff pastry until completely enclosed and all of puff pastry is used. Seal seam with your fingers. Transfer to baking sheet, seam-side down, and continue with second roll. Place baking sheet in refrigerator for 1 hour.
9. Preheat oven to 375°F.
10. Remove rolls from refrigerator and brush off any excess flour. Brush each roll with beaten egg, coating all sides. Season each roll with a little salt and pepper. Trim ends so they are even. Cut each roll into 8 pieces, about 1-inch each thick.
11. Coat another baking sheet with cooking spray and place cut rolls upright, with seam-sides down, about 1-inch apart. Bake for about 12-14 minutes, until tops are golden brown.
12. Meanwhile, in a small bowl, combine mayonnaise and crushed red peppers and season with salt and pepper. Adjust spice level to your preference.
13. Transfer to a small serving bowl. Place rolls on a serving platter with hot pepper aioli on the side. Serve warm.

cook's note: I recommend Bom Petisco brand of hot crushed peppers, available at most Portuguese markets.

baked brie with honey + almonds

SERVES 4-6

When you place a dish of warm, melted cheese in front of your guests, conversations stop. Hot from the oven and served with a loaf of freshly toasted bread, this simple appetizer demands to be eaten immediately. Gooey cheese drizzled with a local honey (I love Aquidneck Honey from Rhode Island) and topped with some almonds is all you need to silence a crowd.

1   large French baguette, sliced on a diagonal into 1/2-inch slices
1   13-ounce round brie cheese
2   tablespoons honey
2   tablespoons finely chopped almonds
     Kosher salt, to taste
     Freshly ground black pepper, to taste

1. Preheat oven to 400°F.
2. On a large baking sheet, add bread slices, leaving enough room for baking dish. Set aside.
3. Cut top rind off of brie and discard. Place brie, cut side up, in an oven-safe round baking dish slightly bigger than round of brie itself (see cook's note). Drizzle top of brie with honey, sprinkle with almonds, and season with salt and pepper. Place baking dish on baking sheet with bread and bake for about 5 minutes. Turn bread slices over and return baking sheet to oven and bake until bread is golden brown, about 5 minutes more. Carefully remove bread slices and transfer to a serving plate. Return baking sheet with baking dish of brie to oven and continue baking until edges of cheese start to bubble and turn golden brown and cheese is melted, another 10 minutes. Carefully transfer dish with brie to serving plate. Serve warm with bread slices.

cook's note: You can use any size brie for this recipe, just be sure the baking dish you put it in isn't much bigger than the brie itself or the cheese will lose its shape when it melts. There should be about a 1-inch space between brie and outside of dish.

tuna tartare with sesame

SERVES 8-10

I love to entertain, and creating dishes especially for my guests is something that I always look forward to. A group of my sushi-loving friends inspired this particular appetizer. This delicious, effortless dish is perfect for entertaining because most of the work is done by the time your guests arrive. It's light and refreshing—perfect for a warm summer night with friends.

3/4 pound fresh sushi-grade tuna steak, cut into 1/4-inch dice
2   scallions, white and light green parts, finely minced
1/2 jalapeño, seeded and finely minced
1   tablespoon finely chopped fresh cilantro
2   tablespoons canola oil
     Zest and juice from 1 lime
2   teaspoons soy sauce
1/4 teaspoon toasted sesame oil
     Pinch of kosher salt
24   sesame crackers, for serving
     Sesame seeds, for garnish

1. Place tuna in a medium bowl, add scallions, jalapeño, and cilantro, and toss to combine.
2. In a small bowl, combine oil, lime zest and juice, soy sauce, and sesame oil and season with salt. Pour over tuna and toss to combine.
3. Cover bowl with plastic wrap and refrigerate for about 1 hour to chill and allow flavors to develop.
4. To serve, place a spoonful of tuna mixture on crackers and top with a few sesame seeds for garnish. Serve immediately.

cook's note: When you're buying any type of fish, you can judge its freshness by its smell, or lack thereof. Fresh fish should not smell fishy; in fact it should have very little smell. If possible, buy seafood from a market with a good reputation for selling fish. Fresh tuna should not look dry or have any brown spots on it. For tartare or sushi recipes, ask specifically for sushi-grade fish, and buy it the same day you are planning on using it.

basic crostini

MAKES APPROXIMATELY 20-30 CROSTINI

Crostini, which means "little toasts" in Italian, are the perfect appetizer for a large party. They are great rubbed with a garlic clove and drizzled with olive oil, topped with homemade pesto and freshly grated Parmesan, or served with your favorite jam and cheese. They are one of my favorite appetizers to make when entertaining a crowd because they are so versatile. (What doesn't work on a delicious toasted baguette?)

To make crostini, simply cut 1 large French baguette on a diagonal into 1/2-inch thick slices. Grill (or toast) slices until golden brown on both sides. Add desired toppings and serve.

ricotta + local honey

Smear a generous amount of ricotta on each crostini and drizzle with a bit of local honey. Top with a pinch of salt and pepper and serve.

fresh mozzarella + roasted garlicky tomatoes

Preheat oven to 400°F. Place 2 pints cherry tomatoes, 2 minced garlic cloves, and leaves from 2 fresh thyme sprigs on a baking sheet. Drizzle mixture with about 2 tablespoons of olive oil and season with salt and pepper. Gently toss together until everything is coated. Roast tomatoes, turning occasionally, until they are softened and lightly browned, about 20-25 minutes. To serve, place a piece of fresh mozzarella on each crostini and top with some tomatoes, slightly breaking them up as you go. Drizzle each crostini with a bit of olive oil and season with a pinch of salt and pepper.

fresh pea purée, prosciutto + parmesan

Make pea purée. In a medium saucepan, bring some water to a boil. Add 2 cups peas and cook until bright green, about 3-4 minutes. Drain and place in an ice bath for 3-4 minutes. Add drained peas to a food processor along with 1/4 cup ricotta cheese and season with salt and pepper. Pulse until just combined. With motor running, slowly stream in about 2-3 tablespoons of olive oil and process until smooth (it should be fairly thick when finished). Spread a bit of pea purée onto each crostini. Drizzle additional olive oil on top. Top each with 1/3 piece of a thin slice of prosciutto and a light dusting of freshly grated Parmigiano-Reggiano. Season with salt and pepper and serve.

crostini with wilted kale + goat cheese

MAKES 12 CROSTINI

Here, creamy goat cheese, lemon, and wilted kale perfectly combine for a bite-size appetizer.
I prefer to use a thin, round, seeded baguette (the baguette pictured comes from Seven Stars Bakery
in Providence, RI), cut into 1-inch thick pieces. If you use a wider baguette, pieces should be cut
into 3/4-inch thick slices.

	Baguette, cut into 12 1-inch thick slices
1/4	bunch curly kale, washed and dried
1	tablespoon extra virgin olive oil
1	medium shallot, thinly sliced
	Kosher salt, to taste
	Freshly ground black pepper, to taste
1/2	cup low-sodium vegetable stock
4	ounces goat cheese, softened
	Zest of 1 lemon

1. Preheat oven to 400°F.
2. Place bread slices on a baking sheet and bake until golden brown on both sides, about 5-10 minutes. Set aside.
3. Trim bottoms of kale leaves and discard. Remove and discard inner stems and roughly chop remaining kale into small pieces, about 2-inches in size.
4. In a medium sauté pan, heat oil over medium heat. Add shallot and cook until softened, about 5 minutes. Season with salt and pepper. Add kale and cook until just wilted, about 5 minutes. Add stock to pan and bring to a boil. Cover and reduce heat to medium-low. Continue to cook until kale is tender and wilted, about another 5 minutes.
5. Spread a bit of goat cheese evenly over each slice of bread. Top with kale. Add a pinch of lemon zest on top of each, season with salt and pepper, and serve.

MILK & HONEY BAZAAR

Located in the heart of historic Tiverton Four Corners in Rhode Island, Milk & Honey Bazaar is an artisanal cheese and specialty foods market that is filled with a vast assortment of cheeses for every palate. From local Narragansett Creamery to imported Manchego, the shop carries over one hundred varieties of cheese from all over the world and is always on the hunt for more. Cathi and Gerry Fournier, customers who stepped in when the shop was about to close in December 2010, operate this charming little store.

Whether you're looking for something specific or just want to browse, you will find that Milk & Honey Bazaar encourages its customers to try samples and decide what they like before making a purchase. And they're always happy to offer suggestions. In addition to its wide assortment of cheese, the shop carries everything you need to accompany it, including crackers, baguettes, pâtés, charcuterie, and a great assortment of jams and preserves—everything you need for your party or picnic basket.

SEVEN STARS BAKERY

When Lynn and Jim Williams opened Seven Stars Bakery in January 2001 their mission was relatively simple: bake great stuff and treat customers well.

With the help of a modest staff, Lynn and Jim baked and sold every loaf of bread and pastry from the original Hope Street location in Providence, RI. Their business grew; they started selling to restaurants and grocery stores and quickly expanded their operations to include two other retail cafés and an off-site bakery in Pawtucket. (If you've had a loaf of bread from Seven Stars Bakery, you'll know why their product is in such demand!)

Seven Stars specializes in crusty hearth-style breads and pastries, and they take no shortcuts. Everything is handmade without additives, preservatives, or pre-made fillings. Their breads are available at local markets and some farmers' markets, but the three bakeries (on Hope Street in Providence, another on Broadway, and the third at the Rumford Center in East Providence) are always worth a special trip, especially for one of their completely addictive sticky buns, a cup of hot coffee, and the friendly, warm atmosphere.

chouriço-stuffed mushrooms

SERVES 6-8

Stuffed mushrooms have been popular for decades— and with good reason. These tasty appetizers are so versatile that they can be filled with just about anything. Taking my cue from the Portuguese flavors around me, I add ground chouriço to mine, which gives the mushrooms a subtle smoky flavor.

18 small (or 12 medium-sized) white button mushrooms
1   mild chouriço link, casing removed
3   tablespoons extra virgin olive oil, divided, plus extra for drizzling
1   small onion, finely minced
    Kosher salt, to taste
    Freshly ground black pepper, to taste
1   clove garlic, finely minced
2   tablespoons finely minced fresh flat-leaf Italian parsley
1/2 cup plain breadcrumbs
1/4 cup plus 2 tablespoons low-sodium beef stock

1. Preheat oven to 400°F.
2. Carefully remove stems from mushrooms, taking care to leave round caps intact. Discard stems (or save for a later use). Lightly moisten a paper towel and wipe off any dirt on outside caps of mushrooms. Using a teaspoon, gently scrape out gills inside mushrooms so that they are smooth and easier to fill (do this carefully as to not break mushrooms caps). Brush outer mushroom caps lightly with 1 tablespoon olive oil and place cavity side up on a baking sheet (if mushrooms don't sit flat, trim a tiny piece of outer cap). Set aside.
3. Cut chouriço into 1-inch pieces and place in a food processor. Pulse until chouriço is finely chopped. Set aside.
4. In a non-stick pan, heat 1 tablespoon olive oil over medium heat. Add chouriço and cook until just lightly browned, about 5-7 minutes. Transfer to a medium bowl and set aside. To pan, add remaining 1 tablespoon olive oil. Add onions and cook until softened, about 5 minutes. Season with salt and pepper. Add garlic and cook for another 1-2 minutes. Transfer onion mixture to bowl of chouriço and mix to combine. Stir in parsley.
5. To mixture, add breadcrumbs and toss to combine. Add stock and stir until mixture is well combined and just wet enough to hold together with two fingers (add more stock or breadcrumbs if necessary). Using a teaspoon, carefully place stuffing into cavity of each mushroom, creating a small mound. Drizzle mushrooms and stuffing with olive oil (just enough to lightly cover each mushroom, about 1-2 drops per mushroom) and bake until stuffing is lightly browned, 20-25 minutes. Serve warm.

shrimp toasts with scallions, ginger + sesame

MAKES APPROXIMATELY 18 TOASTS

This flavorful shrimp mixture, speckled with ginger and scallions, makes for a light and easy appetizer that's perfect for entertaining. The mixture should have enough texture so that some larger pieces of the shrimp and vegetables are visible, but chopped enough so that it's still easy to eat as a bite-size appetizer.

1 loaf good-quality white bread
3/4 pound fresh medium shrimp, peeled and deveined
2 scallions, white and light green parts, chopped
2 tablespoons chopped fresh cilantro, plus extra for garnish
1 clove garlic, finely minced
1 1/2 teaspoons soy sauce
1 1/2 teaspoons sesame oil
1 1/2 teaspoons minced ginger
1 large egg white
   Zest from 1 lime
2 tablespoons sesame seeds

1. Preheat oven to 350°F.
2. Cut bread into 1/2-inch thick slices. Using a 2-inch cookie cutter, cut bread into 18 rounds. Set aside.
3. Wash and pat dry shrimp. Chop shrimp into small bite-size pieces, with a bit of texture left to them (see headnote). Place shrimp in a medium bowl.
4. To bowl, add scallions, cilantro, garlic, soy sauce, sesame oil, ginger, egg white, and lime zest and mix together until everything is incorporated.
5. Place a bit of shrimp mixture onto each round of bread, forming mounds. Place rounds on a baking sheet and bake until cooked through and tops of toasts are golden brown, about 10-15 minutes. Remove toasts from oven and turn oven temperature to broil.
6. Sprinkle a few sesame seeds on top of each round, place toasts back under broiler, and cook until tops of shrimp toasts are browned and seeds are lightly toasted, 30 seconds to 2 minutes (watch them carefully so they do not burn).
7. Remove toasts from oven and transfer to a serving platter. Garnish each toast with a small piece of cilantro and serve warm.

cook's note: If you're cutting the bread into rounds, mound enough mixture onto each piece so that it has some height to it. If you can't find unsliced bread, cut pre-sliced bread into triangles, just be sure the bread is thick enough (1/2-inch thick works well). The thinner the bread, the finer you'll want to make the mixture so it will not overwhelm the bread.

CHEF RECIPE

modern clams casino with oregano mojo

MAKES 12 CLAMS

From Richard Garcia, Executive Chef, 606 Congress, Boston, MA.

I wanted to create a dish that was comfortable but not quite comfort food. When it comes to classic New England dishes, clams casino has been a longtime favorite. Incorporating my Hispanic heritage into this recipe was a must, so both the mojo and chouriço came to mind. A modern version of a New England classic was born and continues to be part of my menus both at home and in the restaurant.

Oregano Mojo

1/4	cup minced fresh oregano
6	cloves garlic, finely minced
	Juice from 2 limes
	Kosher salt, to taste
	Freshly ground black pepper, to taste
1/2	cup extra virgin olive oil

1	cup white wine
12	Topneck Cape Cod clams (see cook's note)
1	mild chouriço sausage link
1	tablespoon extra virgin olive oil
1/4	large Spanish onion, minced
1	clove garlic, finely chopped
1/4	cup finely chopped roasted red peppers
	Juice from 1/2 lemon
1/4	cup Panko breadcrumbs
4	tablespoons unsalted butter, at room temperature
2	tablespoons Grated Landaff Tomme cheese (or Parmigiano-Reggiano)
2	tablespoons minced fresh flat-leaf Italian parsley

1. Make mojo. In a medium bowl, combine oregano, garlic, and lime juice and season with salt and pepper. Stir in olive oil and set aside.
2. In a large saucepan, bring wine and 1 quart water to a boil. Add clams, cover, and cook until clams open, about 3-5 minutes. Transfer clams to a large bowl.
3. Strain cooking liquid through a cheesecloth-lined sieve (or through a fine-mesh sieve) into a bowl and save for another use (this liquid makes great stock for homemade chowder).
4. Shuck clams and mince until coarsely ground. Reserve half of shells and set aside.
5. Remove and discard casing from chouriço and place it in a food processor. Grind chouriço until you have a coarse paste.
6. In a medium sauté pan, heat olive oil over medium heat. Add onions and cook until softened, about 5-7 minutes. Add garlic and cook for another 1-2 minutes. Add chouriço and roasted red peppers and cook until chouriço is browned and cooked through, about another 5-7 minutes. Stir in lemon juice, breadcrumbs, minced clams, butter, cheese, and parsley until well combined. Stuff each reserved clam shell with enough mixture to fill cavity and place on a large baking sheet.
7. Turn on broiler to high and place baking sheet under broiler until tops are golden brown and slightly charred, about 2-3 minutes. Transfer clams to a serving platter, drizzle each with a bit of oregano mojo, and serve.

cook's note: Top Necks are tender, sweet hard-shell clams and are slightly larger than little necks but smaller than cherrystones.

THE COASTAL WINE TRAIL

Wine has been made in New England for centuries, but in recent years there are more wineries making better wines, with some of the most remarkable coming from the Southeastern New England Wine Growing Appellation.

The best way to discover the diverse wines of Southern New England is to a take a scenic road trip on the Coastal Wine Trail. The heart of this wine trail stretches from Cape Cod and the Islands through the South Coast of Massachusetts, coastal Rhode Island, and coastal Connecticut. It is made up of nine vineyards and wineries including Coastal Vineyards, Greenvale Vineyards, Langworthy Farm, Newport Vineyards, Running Brook Vineyards, Sakonnet Vineyards, Travessia Winery, Truro Vineyards, and Westport River Vineyard (see page 11). The entirety of the trail can be visited over the course of two or three days, and you can expect to sample a variety of premier white and sparkling wines.

In addition to the breathtaking landscapes and delicious wines, the Coastal Wine Trail offers a chance to understand the viniculture of this region. Specifically, how this brisk grape-growing region's proximity to the Atlantic Ocean, the warm Gulf Stream waters in the summer and fall, and the position of the coastline allow these vineyards to produce quality wines year after year.

The wineries offer tours, tastings, and jazz concerts, as well as many other special events throughout the year, each in its own idyllic setting.

grilled flank steak with fresh rosemary

chapter 6

from the grill

grilled oysters:

   mignonette sauce

   spicy sriracha butter

   casino style

tomato toasts with serrano ham

grilled flank steak with fresh rosemary

grilled leg of lamb with greens + lemon yogurt

backyard bbq chicken

turkey burgers with smoky chipotle ketchup

grilled chicken with fresh oregano vinaigrette

grilled heirloom tomato + mozzarella pizza

homemade pizza dough

burgers with aged cheddar + homemade tomato jam

grilled hot dogs with spicy beer mustard

grilled radicchio with great hill blue + walnuts

grilled corn with jalapeño-lime butter

grilled oysters with spicy sriracha butter

I love to cook on the grill,
not only because it gets me
outside from dawn until dusk, or because
of the flavor it imparts to the food—just
about everything tastes better with a little
char on it—but also because cooking
outside is usually about gathering friends
and family together. The food is simpler,
and at the height of summer, when cooking
indoors can seem like a punishment, the
ease of preparing meals in the open air is
not only refreshing, but also a pleasure. If
you're like me, these recipes will have you
firing up your grill long before Memorial Day
and well after Labor Day.

grilled oysters

In this region, we are blessed with some of the best oysters on the planet. From the briny bivalves of Island Creek in Duxbury, MA, to the delicate Moonstones from Point Judith, RI, our biggest problem is choosing which variation to try next. On Cape Cod, I almost always go right to Wellfleet for my oysters, but Quivet Neck in Dennis and Wiannos from Cotuit are also showstoppers. Further south, I seek out oysters from Quonset Point and Watch Hill in Rhode Island, and from Stonington and Mystic in Connecticut. If you come across the amazing oysters from Cuttyhunk (see page 163) give those a try.

While many New Englanders would argue that our local oysters are best eaten raw with nothing but the seawater in the shell to garnish them, they are also wonderful when grilled.

Prepare oysters. Rinse under cold water with a stiff brush to remove any dirt (especially at hinge).

Once cleaned, place an oyster in a thick cloth with hinge closest to you. Insert tip of an oyster knife as far into hinge as it will go, wiggling it around until you feel it slip into the shell. With the tip of your knife still inside the oyster, carefully run it between the shells (this will take some practice, so be patient). Twist knife gently to pry open shell. Run knife underneath the oyster to detach it, leaving it in its shell and keeping as much liquid inside as possible. Place oyster onto a bed of crushed ice or rock salt and continue with remaining oysters (discarding top halves of oyster shells as you go).

Preheat grill to high. Shuck as many oysters as you can keep track of on the grill at one time (it's better to work in small batches so they don't overcook). Place shucked oysters carefully on grill, cover, and cook until just warmed through, about 2-3 minutes.

You can also grill the oysters unshucked. To do so, place cleaned oysters on the grill, cover, and cook for 2-3 minutes, checking often, until the top shell begins to loosen. Remove from the grill, carefully open, and serve.

The following toppings will be enough for a dozen oysters. The mignonette sauce will also work with raw oysters.

mignonette sauce

1   shallot, finely minced
1/3   cup champagne or white wine vinegar
1   teaspoon sugar
      Freshly ground black pepper, to taste
1   teaspoon finely minced fresh flat-leaf Italian parsley

1. Place shallots, vinegar, and sugar in a small saucepan and bring to a boil. Cook uncovered for about 3 minutes.
2. Remove from heat and allow to cool.
3. Add pepper and parsley, spoon a small drizzle of mignonette sauce over oysters, and serve.

spicy sriracha butter

4   tablespoons unsalted butter, at room temperature
1   teaspoon Sriracha sauce, or to taste
      Zest of 1/2 lime
      Kosher salt, to taste
      Freshly ground black pepper, to taste

1. In a small bowl, combine butter, Sriracha sauce, and lime zest and season with salt and pepper. Mix until well combined. Taste and add in a bit more Sriracha sauce if desired. Transfer to a serving bowl and allow to set in refrigerator for about 30 minutes.
2. When ready to serve, place a small dollop of butter on top of warm oysters and serve.

casino style

2   slices thick-cut bacon, chopped
4   tablespoons unsalted butter, at room temperature
1   small shallot, finely minced
1   clove garlic, finely minced
      Zest from 1/2 lemon
      Kosher salt, to taste
      Freshly ground black pepper, to taste
1   tablespoon finely minced fresh flat-leaf Italian parsley

1. In a medium sauté pan, cook bacon until crispy. Remove with a slotted spoon, transfer to a plate lined with paper towels, and set aside.
2. In a small bowl, combine butter, shallot, garlic, and lemon zest and season with salt and pepper.
3. Line a baking sheet with aluminum foil and place shucked oysters evenly on top. (If they don't sit straight up, place a small amount of kosher salt under each one to secure them.) Top each oyster with a bit of seasoned butter, followed by a bit of bacon. Place baking sheet on hot grill, close, and grill until butter starts to melt and oysters are warmed through, about 2-3 minutes.
4. Remove oysters from grill and transfer to serving plate filled with rock salt (or kosher salt), nestling oysters in salt to secure them in place. Scatter parsley over top of oysters and serve warm.

tomato toasts with serrano ham

SERVES 4

This simple dish is typically served at the beginning of any good tapas meal. It's a perfect appetizer for entertaining in late summer. I love to grill the bread, which adds a nice smoky flavor to the dish, but you can toast it in the oven as well. Fresh garden tomatoes, some Serrano ham, and a drizzle of a quality olive oil are all you need for easy backyard entertaining.

1   French baguette, cut in half lengthwise
    Extra virgin olive oil, for drizzling
1   large tomato, cut in half crosswise
    Kosher salt, to taste
    Freshly ground black pepper, to taste
8   slices Serrano ham, thinly sliced

1. Preheat grill to medium heat.
2. Drizzle cut sides of each half of bread with a bit of olive oil. Place bread cut side down on grill. Grill until lightly charred, about 3-4 minutes. Turn bread over and cook for another 1-2 minutes. Remove bread and transfer to a large cutting board.
3. Rub cut side of one half of tomato over one half of baguette until flesh is just about gone. Discard tomato. Repeat with remaining tomato and other half of bread.
4. Drizzle each bread half with additional olive oil and season with salt and pepper. Top each half with equal slices of Serrano ham. Cut each half into equal portions and serve.

cook's note: Serrano ham is typically available at gourmet shops (locally, I go to Sid Wainer & Son's Gourmet Outlet, see page 103). If you have trouble finding Serrano ham, prosciutto will work as well.

grilled flank steak with fresh rosemary

SERVES 4-6

Flank steak is a straightforward, flavorful cut of meat. It's best marinated—the longer the better. Marinating the meat overnight not only produces a delicious dinner, it also frees up time, which is helpful when cooking for a crowd.

1   flank steak (about 1 1/2-2 pounds)
1   shallot, roughly chopped
2   garlic cloves, roughly chopped
2   tablespoons chopped fresh rosemary
1   tablespoon Dijon mustard
1/4 cup balsamic vinegar
     Kosher salt, to taste
     Freshly ground black pepper, to taste
1/2 cup extra virgin olive oil, plus extra for grilling

1. Trim and discard any excess fat from steak.
2. Place shallot, garlic, rosemary, mustard, and vinegar in a blender and season with salt and pepper. Purée until well combined. Remove center piece from top of blender and, with machine running, slowly stream in 1/2 cup olive oil and purée until combined. Add more oil if necessary.
3. Place steak in a glass or ceramic baking dish and pour 3/4 of marinade over top of steak (place remaining marinade into a serving bowl, cover, and refrigerate until ready to serve steak). Gently turn steak over in dish, coating meat on all sides with marinade. Cover with plastic wrap and refrigerate for at least 4 hours, turning once.
4. Preheat grill to medium heat. Fold a paper towel into quarters and coat one side with 2 tablespoons olive oil. Place paper towel in tongs and brush oiled side of towel onto grill grates to coat. Discard paper towel.
5. Remove steak from marinade, wipe off any excess liquid, and season both sides of steak with salt and pepper. Grill, covered, until grill marks form, about 5-7 minutes. Turn steak and continue grilling until cooked through, another 5-7 minutes. Transfer steak to a cutting board, tent with aluminum foil, and allow to rest for 5-10 minutes. Slice steak across grain and serve with reserved dressing.

grilled leg of lamb with greens + lemon yogurt

SERVES 4

I try to grill all year round, but sometimes the piles of snow and icy steps that come with a New England winter keep me inside until the thaw. Regardless of the weather, by Easter I'm ready to get out there and this is my favorite recipe to make for the holiday. Grilling the lamb gives the meat a flavorful char and plenty of crispy edges (my favorite part). A butterflied, boneless leg of lamb (ask your butcher to do this for you) makes for easy entertaining. I serve this dish family-style with beautiful, fresh greens over the top. The lemon yogurt sauce is light and refreshing and pairs well with the traditional flavors of the lamb.

4 cloves garlic, minced
2 tablespoons (about 1 sprig) finely chopped fresh rosemary
¼ cup red wine vinegar
¼ cup plus 2 tablespoons extra virgin olive oil, plus extra for drizzling
   Kosher salt, to taste
   Freshly ground black pepper, to taste
2½ pounds boneless leg of lamb, butterflied

Lemon Yogurt
12 ounces plain Greek yogurt
   Zest and juice from 1 lemon
2 tablespoons extra virgin olive oil

   Fresh arugula (or mixed greens), for serving

1. In a large baking pan, combine garlic, rosemary, red wine vinegar, and olive oil and season with salt and pepper. Add lamb, coating entirely with marinade on both sides. Cover with plastic wrap and refrigerate overnight, turning at least once while it marinates.
2. Remove lamb from marinade and allow to sit at room temperature for 15-20 minutes.
3. Preheat grill to medium-high heat.
4. Lower heat on grill to medium and place lamb on grill. Cook until internal temperature is 125°F (for rare), or 135°F (for medium rare), about 8-10 minutes per side. Remove from grill, tent with aluminum foil, and allow to rest for 15-20 minutes before slicing.
5. Meanwhile, make lemon yogurt. In a medium bowl, combine yogurt, lemon zest, and juice, season with salt and pepper, and stir in olive oil. Transfer to a small serving bowl and set aside.
6. Slice lamb into ½-inch thick pieces on a diagonal and place on a serving platter. Scatter arugula over top of lamb, drizzle with a bit of olive oil, season with salt and pepper, and serve with lemon yogurt sauce on the side.

PERSIMMON PROVISIONS

Though many know Chef Champe Speidel and his wife, Lisa, as the dynamic duo behind the exquisite restaurant Persimmon in Bristol, RI, few may know that Champe was a butcher for ten years before attending Johnson & Wales University. As their restaurant began to grow, it became increasingly difficult to butcher as much as Champe wanted to—his restaurant simply had too little counter space for him to practice his first craft.

In November 2010, Champe and Lisa opened Persimmon Provisions, a butchery and artisanal food shop in picturesque Barrington, RI, to fix that problem. This charming little shop allows Champe to break down and butcher whole animals from farms that specialize in locally and humanely raised meats—and more to the point, gives him the opportunity to take full advantage of every part of the animal. If you are seeking a hard-to-find cut, or want to explore overlooked delicacies that come from artful butchery, this is your place.

Persimmon Provisions sells as much local product as they can, but what concerns the Speidels most are farming practices and how animals are raised. They pride themselves on being purveyors of high quality products. In addition to meats and charcuterie, the shop also sells a nice selection of sauces and stock, gourmet cheeses, jams and jellies, olive oils and vinegars, and a smattering of food prepared by the Persimmon kitchen.

backyard bbq chicken

SERVES 4

The aroma of grilled chicken slathered in a sweet and sticky barbecue sauce is the telltale of a great backyard party. To help keep this chicken moist, I brine it first. It's important to cook the chicken slowly over medium heat (or lower) and stay close by, especially when you first put the chicken on the grill. If the grill is too hot, it will quickly burn the skin. The cut of chicken you use is up to you, but I prefer chicken breasts. If you use a different cut, be sure to adjust the cooking time.

Brine
1/4 cup kosher salt
1/4 cup light brown sugar
2 cloves garlic, crushed
Water, enough to cover chicken
4 bone-in, skin-on chicken breasts

BBQ sauce
1 tablespoon extra virgin olive oil, plus extra for grilling
1 small onion, finely diced
Freshly ground black pepper
4 cloves garlic, finely minced
3/4 cup ketchup
1/2 cup light brown sugar
1/2 cup apple cider vinegar
1/4 cup molasses
2 tablespoons Dijon mustard
2 tablespoons Worcestershire sauce

1. Make brine by combining salt, sugar, garlic, and water in a large glass bowl. Add chicken, cover with plastic wrap, and refrigerate for 1 hour.
2. Make BBQ sauce. In a medium saucepan, heat 1 tablespoon olive oil over medium heat. Add onion, cook until softened, about 5 minutes, and season with salt and pepper. Add garlic and cook for another 1-2 minutes. Add remaining BBQ sauce ingredients and whisk to combine. Bring to a gentle boil, reduce heat to low, and cook, stirring occasionally, until sauce has thickened slightly, about 15-20 minutes. Transfer 1/2 of sauce to a small bowl (to be used for basting) and leave remaining sauce on low heat.
3. Remove chicken from brine and pat dry completely. Discard brine.
4. Preheat grill to medium heat. Fold a paper towel into quarters and coat one side with 2 tablespoons of olive oil. Place paper towel in a pair of tongs and brush oiled side of towel onto grill grates to coat. Discard paper towel.
5. Brush chicken with olive oil and season with salt and pepper. Grill chicken skin-side down until a light char forms, about 5 minutes (if skin is cooking too quickly, lower heat to medium-low). Flip chicken, baste skin-side with BBQ sauce, and cook for another 10 minutes. Flip chicken, basting again, and cook for another 5 minutes. Flip again, baste, and continue cooking until chicken is cooked through, another 3-5 minutes (about 20-25 minutes total).
6. Transfer chicken to a cutting board, tent with aluminum foil, and let rest for 5-10 minutes. Transfer warm BBQ sauce to a serving dish and serve with chicken.

turkey burgers with smoky chipotle ketchup

MAKES 6 BURGERS

Ground turkey makes a healthier alternative to a traditional beef burger, and these delicious burgers pair wonderfully with the smoky chiptole ketchup. You can find chipotle chiles in many gourmet markets. The small cans come in 2 varieties: chipotle chiles in adobo sauce and chipotle salsa. In the adobo sauce version, most of the heat is in the actual chiles, so be sure to adjust the amount you use based on how spicy you want it to be. The salsa version is puréed and has a nice smoky flavor.

2   pounds ground turkey
2   tablespoons finely minced fresh cilantro
2   tablespoons finely minced fresh flat-leaf Italian parsley
1/2 teaspoon ground cumin
    Kosher salt, to taste
    Freshly ground black pepper, to taste
    Vegetable oil, for greasing

Smoky Chipotle Ketchup
3-4 tablespoons chipotle salsa (or chipotle chiles in adobo sauce)
3-4 tablespoons ketchup

6   slices Monterey (or Pepper) Jack cheese
6   small hamburger rolls, split

1. Preheat grill to medium heat.
2. In a large bowl, combine turkey, cilantro, parsley, and cumin and season with salt and pepper. Gently mix until ingredients are incorporated. Divide mixture into 6 equal portions.
3. Using wet hands, form mixture into 6 burgers, taking care not to overwork meat. Using your thumb, create a small indention in middle of each burger (this allows them to cook evenly and helps them keep their shape while they cook) and season indented side of each burger with salt and pepper.
4. Brush both sides of burgers with a thin layer of vegetable oil and season one side of each with salt and pepper. Grill burgers, seasoned-side down, for 4-5 minutes. Flip and cook until cooked through, about another 2-3 minutes.
5. Meanwhile, in a medium bowl combine 3 tablespoons chipotle salsa and ketchup and season with salt and pepper. Taste for seasoning, adjust level of heat as desired (add more chipotle if you want it spicier, or more ketchup if it's too hot). Set aside.
6. When burgers are almost done, top each with 1 slice of cheese, close grill, and cook until cheese melts. Place rolls cut side down on grill and cook until grill marks form, 1-2 minutes. Remove rolls and place on individual serving plates or a large serving platter. Place burgers on bottom of each roll, top each with desired amount of chipotle ketchup, and serve.

grilled chicken with fresh oregano vinaigrette

MAKES 1 CHICKEN

This recipe is a version of "chicken under a brick." Because the chicken is flattened on the grill, the skin becomes very crispy—which is the best part. A tart, flavorful vinaigrette serves as both a marinade and a delicious finish to the dish.

Fresh Oregano Vinaigrette
- 1/4 cup sherry vinegar
- 4 cloves garlic, finely chopped
- 2 tablespoons finely chopped fresh oregano
- 1 tablespoon Dijon mustard
- Kosher salt, to taste
- Freshly ground black pepper, to taste
- 1/4 cup plus 2 tablespoons extra virgin olive oil

- 1 whole chicken, approximately 3-4 pounds, deboned and butterflied (see cook's note)

1. Make vinaigrette. In a medium bowl, combine vinegar, garlic, oregano, and mustard and season with salt and pepper. Slowly whisk in olive oil to emulsify. Reserve 1/4 of marinade in a small bowl; cover with plastic wrap and refrigerate.
2. Pat chicken completely dry. Place chicken in a large baking dish and cover with remaining marinade, coating both sides. Cover with plastic wrap and refrigerate for at least 4 hours, turning once.
3. Preheat grill to medium heat. Fold a paper towel into quarters and coat one side with 2 tablespoons of olive oil. Place paper towel in a pair of tongs and brush oiled side of towel onto grill grates to coat. Discard paper towel.
4. Cover a brick entirely with aluminum foil and set aside.
5. Remove chicken from marinade, wiping off excess, and season both sides with salt and pepper. Place chicken skin-side down on grill and top with brick. Cook until nice grill marks form, about 5-10 minutes. Using a pair of tongs and a spatula, carefully remove brick and flip chicken. Return brick to top of chicken until cooked through, about 10-15 minutes. Remove brick and set aside. Remove chicken, place skin-side up on a cutting board, and tent with aluminum foil. Allow to cool slightly before serving, about 10 minutes.
6. Cut chicken into pieces, transfer to a large serving plate, and drizzle with reserved vinaigrette. Scatter a few sprigs of fresh oregano over top and serve.

cook's note: Most butchers will debone and butterfly a whole chicken for you.

grilled heirloom tomato + mozzarella pizza

SERVES 4-6

Making pizza on the grill is a sure sign of summer; it's easy, fun, and delicious. There are a few things to keep in mind, however. Lightly oil both sides of the dough or it will stick to the grates. Additionally, pizza dough tends to cook quickly so stay close. (Depending on your grill, it may take more or less time than what I recommend.) Lastly, it's important to divide the dough into smaller, more manageable portions so they are easier to flip. (Trying to grill an entire large dough at one time will definitely cause you some despair…trust me). If time allows, try making your own dough from scratch. If you don't have time, purchase dough from your favorite pizza shop; most will sell just the dough if you ask.

4   tablespoons extra virgin olive oil, divided, plus extra for serving
1   buffalo mozzarella ball
    Flour, for dusting
1   prepared pizza dough, cut in half
    Kosher salt, to taste
    Freshly ground black pepper, to taste
1   large heirloom tomato, thinly sliced
    Fresh hand-torn basil, for serving

1. Preheat grill to medium heat. Fold a paper towel into quarters and coat one side with 2 tablespoons of olive oil. Place paper towel in a pair of tongs and brush oiled side of towel onto grill grates to coat. Discard paper towel. Pour remaining 2 tablespoons olive oil in a small bowl.
2. Pat dry mozzarella, removing any excess moisture, cut into slices, about 1/4-inch thick, and set aside.
3. On a lightly floured surface, gently stretch each piece of dough into a circle, trying to get dough thin enough so that you can almost see through it, but taking care not to tear it or make a hole in it.
4. Using a pastry brush, brush top side of each piece of dough with a thin layer of olive oil and season with salt and pepper. Transfer one piece of dough onto a pizza peel (or cutting board) and then place onto grill, oiled-side down. Cook until lightly charred, 3-5 minutes, or until bottom releases easily from grill (if dough is cooking too quickly, turn temperature down).
5. While pizza cooks, brush top side of dough with olive oil.
6. Using a pair of tongs, flip dough; add 1/2 of mozzarella evenly over top of dough. Close grill, cook until cheese is melted, another 3-5 minutes.
7. Remove pizza from grill, top with half of heirloom tomato slices, and season with salt and pepper. Scatter top of pizza with fresh basil and finish with a drizzle of olive oil.
8. Repeat procedure with remaining pizza dough and serve warm.

homemade pizza dough

YIELDS 2 PIZZA CRUSTS

1   package (2¼ teaspoons) active dry yeast
1   teaspoon sugar
1   cup warm water (110°F)
1   cup "00" Italian flour
2   cups flour
1   teaspoon salt
1   tablespoon extra virgin olive oil, plus extra for greasing

1. In bowl of an electric stand mixer fitted with a dough hook, combine yeast, sugar, and warm water by stirring slightly with a fork. Allow mixture to stand until yeast is activated and starts to foam, about 10 minutes (you will start to smell yeast).
2. Meanwhile, in a medium bowl, combine flours and salt.
3. Grease a medium glass bowl with olive oil until lightly coated on all sides and bottom and set aside.
4. Turn mixer on to low and add in 1 tablespoon olive oil. Slowly add in flour mixture a little at a time, mixing on low speed until all of flour is incorporated, scraping it off dough hook, sides, and bottom of bowl as necessary. When flour is fully incorporated, turn mixer to medium-low and mix until dough comes together into a ball on dough hook (if dough is still a bit crumbly, add warm water, 1 tablespoon at a time, until it comes together).
5. Transfer dough to a floured surface and knead until dough is soft and smooth (dough will go from sticky to smooth). Form into a ball, place dough in greased bowl, and cover with a clean, slightly dampened dishtowel. Place bowl in a warm, draft-free location and allow to rise until doubled in size, about 1 hour.
6. When dough is ready, remove from bowl and turn out onto a floured surface. Using a sharp knife, divide dough into 2 equal portions.
7. If using dough immediately, turn oven on to 425°F and form into disc(s). (If grilling pizza, preheat to medium-high heat.)
8. If freezing dough, coat dough ball(s) with flour and place in a freezer bag, removing as much excess air as possible before sealing. Dough can be kept in freezer for up to 1 month. Transfer frozen dough from freezer to refrigerator at least 8 hours before you want to use it.

cook's note: I prefer to use a combination of both regular flour and "00" Italian flour for my pizza dough. The "00" flour is very finely ground and adds a supple texture to the finished dough, similar to the style of pizza you would find in Naples, Italy. It's readily available at Whole Foods or any good local Italian market.

burgers with aged cheddar + homemade tomato jam

MAKES 6 BURGERS

In addition to starting with the best quality meat, the key to making a good burger is to put it on the grill and leave it alone. Resist any and all temptation to move it around or press it down against the grates. Put it on the grill and wait for the bottom to get a nice crust on it. When it does, the burger will be ready to flip. Topped with melted cheese and a dollop of this mustardy-based tomato jam, it's pure burger bliss.

Tomato Jam
- 4 medium Roma tomatoes, finely diced
- 2 tablespoons sugar
- 2 tablespoons Dijon mustard
- 1 tablespoon white wine vinegar
  Kosher salt, to taste
  Freshly ground black pepper, to taste
  Pinch crushed red pepper flakes, or to taste (up to 1/4 teaspoon)

- 2 pounds ground beef
- 6 ounces aged sharp cheddar, sliced
- 6 small sourdough hamburger rolls, split

1. Make tomato jam. In a medium, non-reactive saucepan, add ingredients and bring to a boil. Reduce heat to simmer for 45 minutes to 1 hour, stirring fairly often to prevent jam from sticking to bottom of pan. When mixture has thickened, remove from heat and allow to cool to room temperature. Transfer to a serving bowl and set aside.
2. Preheat grill to medium heat.
3. Loosely form ground beef into 6 burgers, taking care not to overwork meat. Using your thumb, create a small indention in middle of each burger (this allows them to cook evenly and helps them keep their shape while they cook) and season indented side of each burger with salt and pepper.
4. Place burgers on grill, indented sides down, and allow them to cook, without touching or flattening them, for 4-5 minutes on one side. When burgers release easily from grill, flip and continue cooking until almost done, another 2-3 minutes.
5. Top each burger with equal amounts of cheese, close grill, and cook until cheese melts, another 1-2 minutes. Remove burgers and loosely tent with aluminum foil.
6. Place rolls cut side down on grill and cook until grill marks form, 1-2 minutes. Remove rolls and place on individual plates or a large serving platter. Place burgers on bottom of each roll, top with some tomato jam, and serve.

cook's note: Roma tomatoes are the best choice for this recipe because they aren't overly juicy and they keep their shape in the jam. Other varieties of tomatoes will work but produce a lot more juice. If you are not using Romas, get the jam nice and thick and strain it. The finer you dice the tomatoes for the jam, the smoother it will be. Leftover jam makes a great condiment for sandwiches—especially grilled cheese— or serve it over a piece of fresh fish. It will keep for up to 1 week in the refrigerator.

from the grill   137

blackbird farm, smithfield, ri

I visited Blackbird Farm on a warm day in the middle of July. My friend David Dadekian, Blackbird Farm's resident chef, introduced me to Ann Marie Bouthillette, the passionate and committed owner of this exceptional 150-acre, family-run cattle farm.

Even though Ann Marie grew up in a farming family, it doesn't appear that becoming one of New England's finest producers of Black Angus beef was always in her future. When she and her husband, Kevin were married in 1984, they decided to buy some small feeder animals for themselves. Their three children showed the animals at fair grounds around the region. Some years later, the family decided to purchase cattle the children could develop over several breeding generations—and it was this decision that led the Bouthillette family to purchase their first Black Angus cows.

High quality cows come with a steep price, though, and keeping the cows became exceedingly expensive. When the family faced the hard reality that they would have to sell their cows, luck stepped in. The Bouthillettes received a listing from Farm Fresh Rhode Island about chefs looking for local beef, pork, and chicken. Ann Marie quickly followed up and immediately received four responses from restaurants requesting their Black Angus beef.

As Ann Marie showed me around, I was struck by how beautiful the animals are. These cows have smooth, shiny, black coats, bright eyes, and tails that flop playfully in the summer breeze. These are happy-looking, healthy animals because Ann Marie and Kevin carefully consider every detail in their lives. From breeding and genetics, to the grass they eat and the grains they're fed, these pedigreed Black Angus cows (and the American Heritage Berkshire pigs the Bouthillettes also keep) are well cared for.

The goal at Blackbird Farm is to humanely produce high quality beef with a consistently juicy, tender flavor. The cows give birth at nine months of age. About forty days later, the calves are weaned and raised on pasture. Their grass diet is supplemented as needed with grain, including milled corn, hay, and essential minerals. No hormones are ever injected or fed to the animals.

Blackbird Farm processes the steers between the ages of fifteen and eighteen months at a USDA-inspected and certified humane facility. Each carcass is dry aged for twenty-one days to ensure tenderness and flavor before being shipped directly to some of the best restaurants and markets in Southern New England. The beef is also butchered at the facility and individual cuts are quick-frozen for sale to the public at their farm stand.

Today the farm is able to sustain itself and cover its costs. And because of these conscientious efforts, Blackbird Farm's products are in high demand from the area's best chefs and an increasing following of (very) loyal customers.

grilled hot dogs
with spicy beer mustard

SERVES 4-8

Hot summer days and hot dogs go hand in hand—but what really makes a perfect hot dog is a good, spicy mustard. Make sure to start preparing this one a few days in advance.

Spicy Beer Mustard
1/2 cup yellow mustard seeds
1/4 cup apple cider vinegar
3/4 cup plus 2 tablespoons dark beer, divided
3 tablespoons light brown sugar
3 tablespoons honey
1/2 teaspoon Kosher salt
1/4 teaspoon turmeric
1/8 teaspoon ground allspice

4 tablespoons unsalted butter
8 all-beef hot dogs
8 hot dog buns

1. In a small bowl, cover mustard seeds with apple cider vinegar and 1/4 cup of beer. Cover bowl with plastic wrap and place in refrigerator for about 8 hours, or overnight.
2. In a small saucepan, combine remaining 1/2 cup plus 2 tablespoons beer, brown sugar, honey, salt, turmeric, and allspice. Bring to a boil for 1 minute. Remove from heat and allow to cool, 5-10 minutes.
3. Add cooled liquid to a blender along with soaked mustard seeds (seeds should have absorbed all liquid) and purée until almost smooth. Transfer to a glass jar, cover with plastic wrap, and refrigerate for at least 8 hours.
4. Preheat grill to medium heat.
5. In a small saucepan, melt butter. Transfer butter to a small dish.
6. Grill hot dogs until warmed through, about 5 minutes. Remove from grill and set aside.
7. Using a pastry brush, butter one side of each roll, place buttered-side down on grill, and cook until toasted, about 2-3 minutes. Butter top sides of each roll. Turn rolls and grill other side for another 2-3 minutes. Remove rolls, and place one hot dog in each one, top with spicy beer mustard and serve.

grilled radicchio with
great hill blue + walnuts

SERVES 4

This dish is a great accompaniment to grilled steak. To make a heartier version of this salad as a main course, chop the grilled radicchio after it has cooled slightly, toss it with chopped iceberg lettuce, diced pears, and dressing, and serve at room temperature.

1/4 cup walnuts, roughly chopped

Dressing
1 small shallot, finely minced
2 tablespoons balsamic vinegar
1 tablespoon honey
  Kosher salt, to taste
  Freshly ground black pepper
1/4 cup plus 2 tablespoons extra virgin olive oil, divided

1 large head radicchio, cut into quarters through core (see cook's note)
1/2 cup crumbled Great Hill Blue

1. Preheat oven to 425°F.
2. Place walnuts on a baking sheet, toast until golden brown, about 5-10 minutes, and set aside.
3. Make dressing. In a medium bowl, combine shallot, balsamic vinegar, and honey and season with salt and pepper. Slowly whisk in 1/4 cup olive oil until dressing is emulsified and thickened, then set aside.
4. Preheat grill to medium heat.
5. Brush radicchio on all sides with remaining 2 table-spoons olive oil and season with salt and pepper.
6. Grill radicchio until lightly charred on all sides, about 5-10 minutes.
7. Transfer radicchio to a serving plate and pour dressing over top. Scatter blue cheese and walnuts over radicchio and serve warm.

cook's note: Cutting the radicchio lengthwise through the core will keep the leaves attached at the base when you grill it.

great hill blue, marion, ma

In 1985, Tim Stone left his engineering job in Washington D.C. to return home to run his family's century-old dairy farm, located along Buzzard's Bay in Marion, MA. After about a decade of hard work and declining milk prices, it became clear that dairy farming was fraught with challenges. When the local vet finally left the area, Tim decided that was it. He sold off his herd off seventy Guernsey cows.

Longing to find a way to stay on the farm, Tim and his wife Tina began to brainstorm. They talked with local cheesemongers, shop owners, and restaurants. They consulted Howard Morris, a professor of food science and nutrition at the University of Minnesota. They studied cheesemaking, visited New England cheesemakers, and researched the artisanal cheese market. Eventually, the Stones decided to produce blue cheese, and in August 1996, they began making what is now known as Great Hill Blue.

Great Hill Blue is unique in that it is made with non-homogenized, raw cow's milk, resulting in a full-flavored, smooth-tasting cheese. Most blue cheeses in the United States are made with homogenized and pasteurized cow's milk, which is easier to make and takes less time. The process to make Great Hill Blue, however, is anything but quick.

After procuring fresh milk from local farms, raw milk is pumped into Great Hill's cheese vat for processing. Once the milk has reached the proper temperature, the mold, cheese cultures, and a fermentation-derived rennet are added. Upon coagulation, the curd is cut and stirred until reaching the desired consistency, allowing the whey to be drained off. Each cheese is then hand-filled using traditional techniques. The forms are then inverted by hand every forty-five minutes with turning intervals increasing to 180 minutes over the next eighteen hours, which ensures proper whey expulsion and curd structure.

Every wheel is hand-salted and, a few days later, punched with a needle measuring 1/8 of an inch 150 times per side to allow oxygen to enter and facilitate mold development—or those lovely blue veins we all know as the trademark of blue cheese. After that, the wheels are cured for three weeks. The cheese is eventually moved to the aging room for a minimum of 120 days allowing it to develop its unique and distinct flavor.

Great Hill Blue is widely popular throughout and beyond the region, finding its place on tables in some of the country's best restaurants. Perhaps what is most telling is that after only three years, the American Cheese Society awarded Great Hill Blue first place in the blue category, solidifying its place among the best artisanal cheeses in the country.

grilled corn with jalapeño-lime butter

SERVES 4

The minute corn hits the stand, I long to throw it on the grill and top it with butter and a dusting of salt and pepper. But when I want to dress it up, I increase the heat on the grill, carefully peel back the husks, and grill the corn a little longer. Then, I slather on this zesty, flavorful compound butter and top it off with some queso blanco, a farmer's cheese from Narragansett Creamery.

Jalapeño-Lime Butter
1   stick unsalted butter, at room temperature
1   small jalapeño pepper, cut in half, seeded, and finely diced
    Zest from 1/2 lime
    Kosher salt, to taste
    Freshly ground black pepper, to taste

4   ears fresh corn
2   tablespoons extra virgin olive oil
1   lime, cut into wedges for serving
    Queso blanco, crumbled, for serving

1. Make jalapeño-lime butter. In a medium bowl, combine softened butter with jalapeño and lime zest, season with salt and pepper, and mix until everything is combined. Transfer to a serving dish, cover with plastic wrap, and set aside.
2. Pull husks back from corn, keeping them attached at base, and discard inner silk. Push husks back carefully around ears of corn and soak in cold water for at least 10 minutes.
3. Preheat grill to medium heat.
4. Remove butter from refrigerator and allow it to come to room temperature.
5. Fold a paper towel into quarters and coat one side with 2 tablespoons of olive oil. Place paper towel in a pair of tongs and brush oiled side of towel onto grill grates to coat. Discard paper towel.
6. Remove prepared corn from water, pat completely dry, place on oiled grill (in husks), and cook, covered, turning occasionally, until insides of corn are bright yellow and tender, about 10 minutes. To add additional flavor, peel back husks (leaving them attached at base) and grill corn (turning occasionally) until cobs are lightly charred on all sides, about 3-5 minutes.
7. To serve, carefully pull husks back from ears of corn (if they aren't already) and place corn on a serving platter. Season corn with salt and pepper and serve with jalapeño-lime butter, lime wedges, and queso blanco.

cook's note: If you want the butter to be a bit spicier, leave in some of the jalapeño seeds. If you can't find queso blanco, look for Cotija or any other fresh farmer's cheese. Good quality feta will work here as well.

chapter 7

from the sea

east coast cobb salad

baked scallops with toasted breadcrumbs

grilled shrimp with garlic

beer-battered fish tacos with creamy lime guacamole

seared scallops with corn risotto + basil oil

grilled swordfish + potatoes with thyme-infused mayonnaise

steamed fish with ginger + greens

baked fish with nasturtium butter

shrimp tacos with cucumber salsa

roasted salmon + potato salad with lemon-caper pesto

swordfish kebabs with arugula pesto couscous

mussels with white wine, butter, herbs + sourdough

Seafood, and the industry surrounding it, is part of the fabric of New England. Along the southern coast of the region, where the foodways are at the center of everyday life, there is something reassuring about the sight of fishing boats coming in to dock each day. Those boats represent the region's heritage, a large part of its economy, and its love of life on the water.

New England's annual catch ranks second in the country, only after Alaska's. In fact, Southern New England can lay claim to one of the most prominent ports in the nation today. New Bedford, MA, which was once regarded as the whaling capital of the world, is now one of the largest commercial fishing ports in the United States. Scallops have been the port's saviors, helping New Bedford bring in more revenue than any fishing port in the nation. Smaller—but still significant—ports that line Long Island Sound, Narragansett Bay, and Buzzards Bay also play a huge role in the region's economy and character. And of course, you only have to think of Cape Cod to see how fundamental fishing is to this part of the country, as it was named in the 17th century for the enormous and plentiful codfish found just offshore.

For centuries, rugged New Englanders have taken to the sea to provide for their families. However, recent years have been tough on the region's fishermen, with a seesaw of catch limits and policies that are trying to balance the industry's needs with measures aimed at long-term sustainability. Despite this, there is still an abundance of fresh seafood available throughout the region. Local fish such as scallops, swordfish, cod, and lobster (to name a few) continue to be staples on local tables, and we can only hope that with good practices and smart consumer choices this will be the case for years to come.

east coast cobb salad

SERVES 4

This recipe takes classic elements of a traditional Cobb salad, which originated in California, and adds an East Coast twist. Either steamed or grilled lobsters work here, but I recommend parboiling your lobsters and finishing them on the grill, which gives them a great smoky flavor that goes perfectly with the richness of the avocados and blue cheese. A drizzle of bacon vinaigrette over the top rounds out the flavors and makes this an utterly irresistible dish.

Bacon Vinaigrette

4 thick slices Applewood smoked bacon, diced
2-3 tablespoons Dijon mustard
1 tablespoon white wine vinegar
1-2 teaspoons honey
  Kosher salt, to taste
  Freshly ground black pepper, to taste
1/2 cup extra virgin olive oil

2 1 1/2-2 pound lobsters
2 tablespoons extra virgin olive oil
4 extra large eggs
2 heads romaine lettuce, washed, dried, and cut into bite-size pieces
2 Hass avocados
4 ounces blue cheese, crumbled, or to taste

1. Make vinaigrette. In a large sauté pan, cook bacon until crispy. Remove with a slotted spoon, transfer bacon to a plate lined with paper towels, and set aside. Carefully pour 2 tablespoons bacon grease into a blender, add 2 tablespoons mustard, vinegar, and 1 teaspoon honey, and season with salt and pepper. Remove center from top of blender and, with motor running, stream in olive oil until dressing is combined and emulsified. Taste for seasoning, adding more mustard (if too sweet) or more honey (if too tart) and set aside.

2. Bring a large pot of water to a boil. Add lobsters, cover, and parboil for about 5 minutes, shaking pot occasionally as they cook. (Don't overcook lobsters, as parboiling them just provides a head start.) Carefully remove lobsters from pot and allow them to rest for a few minutes. When cool enough to handle, remove claws and tails (save main body of lobsters for another use). Using a sharp knife (or with a pair of lobster crackers), crack claws once to open up shells and expose meat. Cut open each tail lengthwise from its underside, taking care not to cut completely through shells (tails should open like a book when done).

3. Heat grill to medium-high heat.

4. Brush flesh side of each lobster tail with olive oil and season with salt and pepper. Place lobster tails (flesh-side down) and cracked claws on grill and grill until slightly charred, about 2-3 minutes. Flip and cook for another 2-3 minutes (lobster meat should be opaque when done). Remove and set aside to cool. When cool enough to handle, remove lobster meat from claws and tails and dice.

5. Place eggs in a saucepan and fill with enough cold water to cover eggs by about 1 inch. Bring to a gentle boil; remove from heat. Cover and let stand for 12 minutes. Drain and rinse with cold water. Let stand for 5 minutes, then peel off shells. Roughly chop eggs and set aside.

6. Divide romaine equally among serving dishes.

7. Halve avocado, remove pit, and scoop out flesh. Place each avocado half on cutting board, cut sides down, and dice. Divide avocado among serving dishes, placing on top of romaine.

8. Top each dish with equal parts eggs, bacon, blue cheese, and lobster. Drizzle top of each salad with bacon vinaigrette, season with salt and pepper, and serve immediately.

TURK'S SEAFOOD

Turk's Seafood in Mattapoisett, MA is a classic New England restaurant with a casual, relaxed atmosphere and a reputation for serving the best fish around. This family business was started as a fish market back in the early 80s by the late Richard Pasquill Sr., or "Big Turk." It is now run by Richard Pasquill, Jr. and his family, and it has grown to include a sushi bar and restaurant.

Richard Pasquill, Jr. has been running the operation since his dad, Big Turk, handed him the business right out of high school. "Like most families in the (fish) business, it's about relationships, and we all take care of each other," Pasquill says. And it's these relationships that have served his business well.

Business continues to thrive because of the Pasquill family's extraordinary dedication. For ten months out of the year (Turk's is closed January and February), Pasquill and his staff of about fifty employees work incredibly hard. Long days start early with Pasquill at the fish auction in New Bedford, picking out what he needs for the market and two restaurants.

In 2012, the family gathered to pay tribute to Pasquill, Sr., marking the twentieth anniversary of his death. They renamed the expanded sushi bar Big Turk's Fish and Sake Bar and memorialized him with a portrait painted by local artist Arthur Moniz.

Customers flock to Turk's for local New Bedford scallops, swordfish, and tuna, their most popular items. If you're in the area, make a point to stop at Turk's. Whether you're in the mood for fish and chips, sushi, or the catch of the day, Turk's Seafood has it all.

baked scallops with toasted breadcrumbs

SERVES 4

When entertaining, I love to bake this dish in individual gratin dishes. A simple breadcrumb mixture on top gives it great flavor and contrasts nicely with the scallops' smooth texture.

- 4 tablespoons unsalted butter, at room temperature
- 2 tablespoons extra virgin olive oil, plus extra for drizzling
- 2 small cloves garlic, finely minced
- 1 small shallot, finely minced
- 2 tablespoons finely minced fresh flat-leaf Italian parsley, plus extra for garnish
  Zest from 1/2 lemon
  Kosher salt, to taste
  Freshly ground black pepper, to taste
- 1/4 cup white wine
- 20 sea scallops
- 2 tablespoons freshly grated Parmigiano-Reggiano
- 1/4 cup plain breadcrumbs
  Juice from 1/2-1 lemon

1. Preheat oven to 425°F.
2. Place 4 individual 6-inch round gratin dishes on a baking sheet and set aside.
3. In a medium bowl, add butter, olive oil, garlic, shallot, parsley, and lemon zest, mix until combined, and season with salt and pepper.
4. Place 1 tablespoon wine in bottom of each gratin dish.
5. Remove any tough, crescent-shaped muscle from outside of scallops and discard. Pat scallops dry and place 5 scallops in each dish, grouping them together. Place a dollop of butter mixture on scallops. Scatter equal amounts of Parmigiano-Reggiano over each, followed by breadcrumbs. Drizzle additional oil over top of each dish and season with salt and pepper.
6. Bake until breadcrumbs are lightly toasted, about 10 minutes. Finish under broiler for 1-2 minutes. Drizzle each gratin dish with lemon juice and a bit more parsley and serve warm.

grilled shrimp with garlic

SERVES 4

This recipe is a take on a traditional shrimp and garlic sauce dish that is commonly featured on the menus of Portuguese restaurants throughout Southern New England. The shrimp are typically sautéed, but when I'm at home, I use the same flavors in a grilled version. It is a great starter at a party, as the preparation and cook time is so quick (generally, shrimp cook very quickly, so make sure you're keeping a close eye!).

- 4 metal (or wooden) skewers
- 1 pound extra large shrimp (approximately 16), washed, peeled, and deveined (tails on)
- 1/4 cup extra virgin olive oil
- 1 tablespoon sherry vinegar
- 4 large cloves garlic, finely minced
  Kosher salt, to taste
  Freshly ground black pepper, to taste
- 1/4 cup finely minced fresh flat-leaf Italian parsley, for garnish, optional

1. Soak wooden skewers (if using) in water for at least 30 minutes and set aside.
2. Pat shrimp dry and set aside.
3. In a large bowl, add olive oil, vinegar, and garlic and season with salt and pepper. Stir to combine. Transfer half of marinade to a serving bowl and set aside.
4. Add shrimp to bowl of remaining marinade and toss to coat completely. Cover bowl with plastic wrap and place in refrigerator. Allow shrimp to marinate for 30 minutes.
5. Preheat grill to medium-high heat. Skewer shrimp, dividing them equally among skewers. Discard marinade. Place skewers on grill and cook until shrimp start to turn pink and light grill marks form on bottom, about 1-2 minutes. Turn and continue to cook on other side for 1-2 minutes. Transfer skewers to a serving platter and brush shrimp with reserved marinade. Scatter parsley over shrimp (if using) and serve warm.

beer-battered fish tacos with creamy lime guacamole

SERVES 4-6

Tacos are a perfect dish to serve to a crowd. You can make all the toppings ahead of time, and having your guests assemble their own tacos is a great way to get everyone mingling. The fish is fried in a tempura-like beer batter (see the cook's note for healthier cooking options), which is a nice contrast to the smooth texture of the zesty lime guacamole. Be sure to use thicker, center-cut pieces of white fish when making this dish so they will stand up to the weight of the batter.

1   pound fresh, firm center-cut white fish
    (cod or haddock)

Creamy Lime Guacamole
2   Hass avocados
2   tablespoons chopped fresh cilantro
2   tablespoons sour cream
1/2 jalapeño, seeded and minced
    Juice from 2 limes
    Kosher salt, to taste
    Freshly ground black pepper, to taste

Beer Batter
1 1/2 cups beer (not dark; I like Corona)
1   cup plus 2 tablespoons flour
1   teaspoon chili powder
1   teaspoon salt

8   flour tortillas
    Canola oil, for frying

Toppings
    Red onion, thinly sliced
    Shredded cabbage
    Fresh cilantro, roughly chopped
    Hot sauce
    Fresh limes, quartered

1. Preheat oven to 200°F.
2. Rinse fish and pat dry, cut crosswise into 1-inch-wide strips, and set aside.
3. Make guacamole. Halve avocado, remove pit, and scoop out flesh. Place avocado on a cutting board, cut side down, and dice. Add diced avocado to bowl of a food processor along with cilantro, sour cream, jalapeño, and lime juice, and season with salt and pepper. Blend until smooth and creamy. Refrigerate until ready to serve.
4. Make batter. In a medium bowl, combine beer, flour, chili powder, and salt. Season with pepper. Batter will be thick.
5. Place tortillas on a baking sheet and place in oven to keep warm.
6. Pour about 1 inch of oil into a large, non-stick frying pan with high sides over medium-high heat until oil shimmers and is about to smoke. Using a fork, dip each piece of fish into beer batter, coating all sides. Allow excess batter to drip off. Carefully place fish in oil, a few pieces at a time, and cook until golden, turning as needed to brown on all sides, about 3 minutes per side. Remove fish with a slotted spoon, transfer to a baking sheet lined with paper towels, and season with salt and pepper. Continue with remaining fish.
7. Assemble toppings on a platter.
8. Remove tortillas from oven. Place 1-2 pieces of fish down center of each tortilla, top with some creamy lime guacamole, add desired toppings, and serve.

cook's note: For a healthier option, bake or grill the fish.

To bake: Preheat the oven to 350°F. Toss the fish lightly with lime juice and a bit of olive oil so it won't stick to a baking dish. Sprinkle with a pinch of chili powder and cumin and season with salt and pepper. Bake until cooked through, about 10 minutes.

To grill: Heat grill to medium heat. Place fish in a single layer in aluminum foil and drizzle with a bit of lime juice. Loosely wrap fish completely in foil and place enclosed package on grill. Cook for 5-10 minutes, depending on thickness of fish (when it flakes apart easily, it's done).

seared scallops with corn risotto + basil oil

SERVES 4

I'm always looking for new ways to incorporate garden basil into my cooking, especially at the end of the summer. While pesto is a good option, so are flavored oils. You can make them with any herbs from your garden, and they're a terrific way to finish a dish. Here, basil oil is drizzled over a beautiful dish of seared scallops and fresh corn risotto, adding a few pops of bright green to this light and refreshing meal. The risotto is made from stock rendered from the corn cobs, giving the rice a rich, sweet flavor.

Basil Oil
2   cups fresh basil
1/2   cup extra virgin olive oil

Risotto
2   medium ears corn, husks and silks removed
3   tablespoons unsalted butter, divided
1   shallot, thinly sliced
    Kosher salt, to taste
    Freshly ground black pepper, to taste
1   cup arborio rice
1/2   cup white wine

12   sea scallops
2   tablespoons extra virgin olive oil

1. Make basil oil. Bring a medium saucepan of water to a boil. Submerge basil and blanch for about 15-20 seconds (this will help it hold its color). Drain and rinse basil under cold water, and then pat completely dry with paper towels. Transfer to blender. With motor running, slowly stream in olive oil and purée until smooth. Pour mixture through a fine-mesh sieve into a jar or bottle. Discard solids. Store in a cool, dark place for up to 2 days.

2. Make corn stock. Remove kernels from each ear of corn. One ear at a time, cut off end of cob and stand it straight up. With a sharp paring knife, carefully cut off corn kernels and place in a bowl (there should be about 1 1/2 cups of kernels when finished). Place cobs and 4 cups of water in a large stockpot and bring to a boil. Cover, reduce heat to low, and cook for about 30 minutes. Remove cobs from water and discard. Add 2 more cups water to pot and place over medium heat.

3. Start risotto. In a large saucepan, add 2 tablespoons butter over medium-high heat. Add shallot, cook until translucent, about 5 minutes, and season with salt and pepper. Add rice, stirring in pan to coat with butter and shallots, and cook for 1-2 minutes.

4. Add wine to deglaze, scraping browned bits from bottom of pan. Cook until wine is evaporated, 1-2 minutes. Reduce to medium heat. Add 1/2 cup corn stock, stirring constantly, until almost absorbed. Add another 1/2 cup corn stock and cook until almost absorbed. Repeat two more times until 2 cups of stock have been added. Add corn and another 1 cup of stock and cook until rice is tender and mixture is creamy, about 20-25 minutes (taste rice for texture after 20 minutes). Continue cooking if necessary, adding more stock and stirring as needed.

5. While risotto cooks, prepare scallops. Remove any tough, crescent-shaped muscle from outside of scallops and discard. Pat scallops dry and season one side with salt and pepper.

6. Heat a large, non-stick sauté pan over medium-high heat for 1-2 minutes. Add olive oil and cook until hot but not smoking. Add scallops, seasoned side down, working in batches if necessary to avoid overcrowding pan. Gently press scallops down in pan (this will help them sear evenly). Cook until lightly browned on bottom, about 2 minutes. (Scallops should release easily from pan when they are ready to be turned; if not, continue to cook for another minute.) Turn scallops and cook for another 2 minutes. Transfer scallops to a plate and continue with remaining scallops (if necessary).

7. Remove risotto from heat and stir in remaining 1 tablespoon butter. Divide risotto among 4 shallow serving bowls. Top each serving with 3 scallops, drizzle with basil oil, and serve warm.

grilled swordfish + potatoes with thyme-infused mayonnaise

SERVES 4

One of the discoveries I made when I first moved to the coast was that mayonnaise keeps fish wonderfully moist while it cooks. Here, I spread mayonnaise over swordfish before I grill it. I then pair the fish with a simple smashed potato salad dressed in a subtle thyme-infused mayonnaise, which mimics the flavor of the fish. Grilling the potatoes after they've cooked adds a delicious smoky flavor to the dish that brings it all together.

Thyme-infused Mayonnaise
4   tablespoons extra virgin olive oil, divided
4-5 sprigs fresh thyme (individual sprigs that
    will lay flat in a pan), plus extra for garnish
3/4 cup mayonnaise, divided
    Kosher salt, to taste
    Freshly ground black pepper, to taste

12 new potatoes (with skin on), washed and
    scrubbed clean
2   pounds fresh swordfish steaks, cut into
    4 pieces
    Juice from 1 lemon, for serving

1. Make thyme-infused mayonnaise. In a small sauté pan, heat 2 tablespoons olive oil over medium heat. When oil heats up, add sprigs of thyme in a single layer and cook for 5 minutes. (Take care to ensure oil doesn't burn. If oil gets too hot, turn heat to medium-low.) Remove pan from heat and allow oil to cool to room temperature, with thyme still in it, for at least 30 minutes. Place 1/2 cup mayonnaise in a medium bowl. Remove thyme sprigs from olive oil and discard. Pour infused olive oil into bowl of mayonnaise, whisk until completely combined, season with salt and pepper, and set aside.
2. Place potatoes in a large pot and add a pinch of salt. Cover potatoes completely with cold water and bring to a boil over medium-high heat. Cook until potatoes are easily pierced with a fork, about 25-30 minutes. Drain potatoes and set aside.
3. Meanwhile, preheat grill to medium heat. Fold a paper towel into quarters and coat one side with 2 tablespoons of olive oil. Using a pair of tongs, brush oiled side of paper towel onto grill grates. Discard paper towel.
4. Place remaining 1/4 cup mayonnaise in a small bowl. Using a pastry brush, brush each piece of swordfish on both sides with mayonnaise and season one side of each steak with salt and pepper. Place swordfish steaks on grill, seasoned side down, and cook until cooked through, about 5 minutes per side (or longer depending on thickness of steaks). Remove from grill, tent with aluminum foil, and set aside.
5. Place drained potatoes in a large bowl, toss with remaining 2 tablespoons olive oil, and season with salt and pepper. Place potatoes on grill and cook until lightly charred, about 5-10 minutes.
6. Remove potatoes from grill and allow to cool for 1-2 minutes. Place one potato on a cutting board, and using a fork, gently mash it, taking care not to mash it completely. Repeat with remaining potatoes.
7. Place 3 potatoes in center of each plate and drizzle thyme-infused mayonnaise over each. Top each plate with a piece of swordfish and a squeeze of lemon juice. Scatter a bit of fresh thyme over each, season with salt and pepper, and serve immediately.

CHEF RECIPE

steamed fish with ginger + greens

SERVES 4

From Barbara Lynch, Chef/Founder & CEO, Barbara Lynch Gruppo, Boston, MA.

When sourcing incredible, local fish from New England, I love to cook it simply. Steaming gently cooks the fish while allowing the gorgeous flavors of fresh ginger and Thai basil to permeate. The veggies provide additional flavor, texture, and color. I especially love to make this dish on a hot summer night; it's a healthy, simple dish that's light but packed with flavor—just the way I like to eat that time of year!

1	tablespoon white miso
1½	cups water
1½	pound striped bass (or other white fish), scored on top of skin so that it steams evenly
½	cup Thai basil
1	small piece fresh ginger, peeled and minced
2	Thai chile peppers, seeded and chopped
1	small bunch maitake mushrooms or cinnamon cap mushrooms, stems removed
1	bunch mustard greens (or baby bok choy)
2	scallions, white part only

1. Mix miso with water and set aside.
2. Preheat oven to 325°F.
3. Place miso and water in bottom of steamer (I use a ceramic steamer) and add fish. Cover with a layer of basil, ginger, peppers, and mushrooms, followed by mustard greens (or baby bok choy) and scallions. Cover and steam until fish is cooked, about 25 minutes.

baked fish with nasturtium butter

SERVES 4

I had never eaten nasturtium flowers until chef Todd Heberlein served them at a dinner held at Wilson Farm in Lexington, MA. (Todd has since joined Volante Farms in Needham, MA.) Beautifully speckled throughout a slice of butter atop my fish, the flowers were not only completely gorgeous but also incredibly delicious. When I saw nasturtium flowers at a farmers' market, I was inspired to come up with my own version of that very memorable dish.

Nasturtium Butter

1   stick unsalted butter, at room temperature
    Kosher salt, to taste
    Fresh ground black pepper, to taste
    Zest from 1 lemon
12 nasturtium flower petals, washed and completely dried (see cook's note)

4   4-ounce pieces of cod, haddock, or halibut, each about 1½-inch thick

1. Make butter. Place butter, a pinch of salt and pepper, and lemon zest in a medium bowl. Finely chop nasturtium flower petals and add them to bowl. Using a spatula, gently mix until everything is combined and butter has visible flecks of flowers throughout. Transfer butter mixture onto a piece of plastic wrap and roll into a smooth log shape (like a sausage), twisting up both ends to enclose. Refrigerate until firm, at least 1 hour.
2. Preheat oven to 375°F.
3. Place fish in a large baking dish and add about 2 tablespoons water to bottom of dish. Bake until fish is opaque and cooked through, 10-12 minutes.
4. Meanwhile, remove butter from refrigerator and cut 4 slices from log, measuring ½-inch each. Reserve remaining butter for a later use.
5. Pat bottom of fish to remove any excess moisture. Transfer fish to a serving platter. Place one slice of butter on top of each piece of fish and serve warm.

cook's note: Nasturtium flowers have a sweet, yet peppery, flavor that makes for a very interesting and colorful butter. To clean the flowers, place them in a bowl of water and gently swirl them around to release any dirt. Remove them from water and drain off any excess. Place on a clean tea towel or paper towel until completely dry. The stems of the flowers are also edible, but they tend to be a bit bitter, so I like to use only the flowers' petals for this butter. The butter will keep covered in the refrigerator for up to 3 days.

shrimp tacos with cucumber salsa

SERVES 4

Crisp, crunchy cucumbers make a great main ingredient in this refreshing salsa, which goes extremely well with grilled shrimp. Be sure to serve the tacos with lots of limes for that extra touch of acidity that balances out the flavors.

Cucumber Salsa

1 medium cucumber, peeled, seeded, and diced
1/2 small red onion, finely diced
2 teaspoons ground cumin
2 teaspoons honey
2 teaspoons canola oil
3 limes, divided
    Kosher salt, to taste
    Freshly ground black pepper, to taste
1/4 cup roughly chopped fresh cilantro, plus extra for serving

12 large shrimp (about 3/4-1 pound), peeled, deveined, and tails removed
4 soft taco-sized flour tortillas
    Shredded cabbage, for serving
    Sour cream, for serving

1. Make salsa. In a medium bowl, combine cucumber, red onion, cumin, honey, canola oil, and juice from 1/2 lime, season with salt and pepper, and toss to combine. Gently toss in cilantro and set aside.
2. Preheat grill to medium heat.
3. In a medium bowl, toss shrimp with juice from 1 lime, coating all of shrimp, and season with salt and pepper. Place shrimp on grill and cook until lightly charred and cooked though, about 2 minutes per side. Do not overcook. Remove from grill and set aside.
4. Place tortillas on grill and cook until warmed through, about 1-2 minutes on each side.
5. Cut remaining limes into quarters and place in a serving bowl.
6. Place 3 shrimp down center of each tortilla with some cucumber salsa. Top with cabbage, sour cream, and cilantro, and serve warm alongside lime wedges.

roasted salmon + potato salad with lemon-caper pesto

SERVES 4

This is a variation on a traditional pesto, tossed with fresh baby arugula, warm potatoes, and big flakes of roasted salmon.

8	baby white (or small Yukon gold) potatoes, cut in half, larger ones in quarters
1/4	cup plus 3 tablespoons extra virgin olive oil, divided
	Kosher salt, to taste
	Freshly ground black pepper, to taste
2	pounds fresh salmon, bones removed

Lemon-Caper Pesto
2	lemons, divided
1	tablespoon Dijon mustard
1	teaspoon capers (and a splash of their juice)
1/4	cup minced fresh flat-leaf Italian parsley

Baby arugula, for serving

1. Preheat oven to 400°F.
2. In a medium bowl, toss potatoes with 2 tablespoons olive oil and season with salt and pepper. Place potatoes on a large baking sheet and bake for 15 minutes.
3. Place salmon in center of a piece of aluminum foil, lightly coat with 1 tablespoon olive oil, and season with salt and pepper.
4. Remove baking sheet from oven and toss around potatoes, allowing them to brown on other sides. Carefully push potatoes to one side, place salmon (on aluminum foil) on baking sheet, and return baking sheet to oven. Continue to cook until potatoes are fork tender and salmon is flaky, about 15-20 minutes (cooking time depends on thickness of salmon). If potatoes are done before salmon, transfer them to a large bowl, set aside, and finish cooking salmon.
5. Meanwhile, make pesto. In a small food processor (or by hand in a small bowl) combine juice from 1 lemon, mustard, and capers and season with pepper. With motor running, slowly stream in remaining 1/4 cup olive oil and pulse until combined. Stir in parsley.
6. Cut remaining lemon into wedges and place in a small serving bowl.
7. Pour 1/2 of pesto over warm potatoes and toss to coat them completely. (Do this while potatoes are still warm so they absorb pesto's flavor.)
8. Once salmon has cooled slightly, flake into large pieces and add to bowl of potatoes.
9. Add 4 large handfuls of arugula to bowl and gently toss it all together, taking care not to break up salmon too much (everything should be lightly coated with pesto). Divide mixture equally among serving bowls, placing some salmon on top of each serving. Drizzle each bowl with remaining pesto and serve warm or at room temperature with lemon wedges.

swordfish kebabs with arugula pesto couscous

SERVES 4

Pesto is a great condiment to make when you have an abundance of fresh herbs or greens on hand, including arugula, spinach, and Swiss chard—all of which translate into delicious and inventive pesto. I stir arugula pesto into plain couscous, making a beautifully flecked side dish for these swordfish kebabs.

8   wooden (or metal) skewers

Arugula Pesto
3   cups packed fresh baby arugula, divided
     Juice from 1 lemon, divided
1   clove garlic, roughly chopped
     Kosher salt, to taste
     Freshly ground black pepper, to taste
6   tablespoons extra virgin olive oil, divided

2   pounds fresh swordfish steaks, about 1-inch thick
1   cup water
1   cup couscous
1   lemon, cut into wedges, for serving

1. If using wooden skewers, soak them in water for at least 30 minutes.
2. Make arugula pesto. In a food processor, add 2 cups packed arugula, juice from 1/2 lemon, and garlic and season with salt and pepper. Pulse a few times until mixture is finely chopped. Slowly stream in 2 tablespoons olive oil and process until mixture is combined and set aside.
3. Preheat grill to medium-high heat.
4. Cut swordfish steaks into 1-inch cubes (you should have about 40 cubes from 2 steaks) and place in a large bowl. Toss with 2 tablespoons olive oil and season with salt and pepper. Thread swordfish onto skewers (5 per skewer). Place on grill, until cooked through, about 5 minutes. (Turn skewers over halfway through cooking.)
5. Meanwhile, in a medium saucepan, bring water to a boil. Add couscous and stir. Remove from heat, cover, and let stand until water is absorbed, about 5 minutes. Fluff with a fork, stir in remaining 2 tablespoons olive oil and juice from remaining 1/2 lemon, and season with salt and pepper. Allow to cool slightly.
6. Add pesto to couscous and stir until well combined. Place couscous on a large serving platter and top with swordfish skewers. Scatter remaining 1 cup arugula over top and serve warm with additional lemon wedges.

cook's note: You can usually find swordfish already cut into kebab pieces, but I prefer to buy swordfish steaks and cut them into smaller, uniform pieces myself. It doesn't matter what size you cut them into, just be sure that they are all about equal, so they will cook evenly. Larger pieces will take longer to cook, possibly up to 10 minutes, depending on their size.

DAY TRIPPING: CUTTYHUNK ISLAND

Cuttyhunk is one of the Elizabeth Islands, neatly tucked away in a stretch of sixteen small islands that extend southwest from Cape Cod. Though it's just twelve miles off the coast of New Bedford (and about eight miles west of Gay Head, Martha's Vineyard) this sparsely populated island is void of most modern conveniences. People come here to get away from it all, and it's what you can't do here that makes it so special.

The island, which measures less than six hundred acres, is a premier fishing destination for both bass and bluefish. Its sheltered harbor also makes it a favorite spot for sailors. Many come here for the day, anchor up, and spend some quiet time relaxing on the beach or hiking among some of the island's beautiful trails.

The island is also home to Cuttyhunk Shellfish Farms. Run by Seth and Dorothy Garfield, Cuttyhunk Shellfish Farms has been in business for over thirty years and if you are on the island, stopping by the farm's raw bar to try some freshly shucked oysters is a must. (Better yet, call them from your VHF radio and one of the company's floating raw bar boats—two retrofitted lobster vessels—will deliver to your mooring.) During the summer season, the Garfields also operate Lobsters on the Lawn, a traditional lobster bake dinner that they serve overlooking Cuttyhunk Pond.

Cuttyhunk Island is a destination for anyone looking for some serious quiet. But a trip to Cuttyhunk requires a little planning, as services can be limited. There is a market for provisions, a few small spots to grab a bite, and an ice cream shop. If you plan to stay longer than a day, there are a few accommodations, including the Avalon, a beautiful and idyllic B&B, as well as the charming Cuttyhunk Fishing Club.

FISHERMAN'S MARKET AT OCEANSFLEET FISHERIES

Lars Vinjerud II worked his way up from deckhand to captain on the boats of New Bedford, the largest commercial fishing port in the country. Now, OceansFleet Fisheries, Lars' own business, operates eighteen fishing vessels and distributes seafood around the globe.

Fisherman's Market is located in the OceansFleet processing plant, a facility that includes one million pounds of freezer space and a sixty thousand square foot lobster pool. The market, which was the first wholesale seafood market in the Northeast, supplies the public with the highest quality product at competitive prices, fresh from their own vessels.

Fishing is definitely in the blood of the Vinjerud family. Lars' three children, Leif, Lars III, and Lisa, are part of the business as well, learning the trade from the processing floor on up, just like their father did many years ago.

mussels with white wine, butter, herbs + sourdough

SERVES 2-4

A big bowl of fresh mussels needs little more than a flavorful broth and a loaf of crusty bread on the side. Fresh lemon juice and a fine white wine are the basis for this broth, which is light enough to let the mussels shine.

1¹/₂ pounds mussels
1   tablespoon unsalted butter
1   medium shallot, thinly sliced
1   clove garlic, sliced
¹/₂ cup white wine
    Juice of 1 lemon
2   sprigs fresh thyme, plus extra for garnish
1   bay leaf
    Kosher salt, to taste
    Freshly ground black pepper, to taste
1   loaf of sourdough bread, for serving

1. Remove beards of each mussel (beards are weedy growths attached to hinges of shells) and rinse mussels well under cold water. Discard any open mussels and set aside.
2. In a large pot, melt butter over medium heat. Add shallot and cook until translucent, about 5 minutes. Add garlic and cook for another 1-2 minutes. Add mussels and increase heat to high. When mussels start to open, add wine, lemon juice, thyme, and bay leaf, season with salt and pepper, and bring to a boil. Reduce heat and cover pot. Cook until mussels are fully opened, 5-10 minutes, shaking pot a couple of times while holding down lid with a kitchen towel. (Shaking pot will prevent mussels from sticking to bottom of pot.)
3. Take mussels off heat and discard any that have not opened. Remove thyme stems and bay leaf. Transfer mussels to serving bowls, sprinkle each serving with fresh thyme leaves, and serve warm with sourdough bread.

yankee pot roast

from the hearth

When you live on the coast all year round, there is a natural tendency to cook heartier, more substantial meals when the colder weather arrives, bolstering us against the elements. Like the recipes in the preceding chapters, these recipes capture the spirit of the southern coastline of New England—in an altogether different way. They involve a bit more time in the kitchen, but these robust, honest dishes will fill your home with a welcoming aroma and make staying inside on a cold day a pleasure.

yankee pot roast

SERVES 4-6

Cold New England winters make me crave big pots of stews and soups, but nothing is more traditional than a pot roast. Full of nourishing vegetables and with a sauce made from a quality red wine, this one-pot meal will satisfy even on the coldest of days. It is the perfect Sunday meal, simmering in the oven for hours and filling the air with its hearty aroma.

$1/4$	cup extra virgin olive oil
1	$3^3/_4$-pound boneless beef chuck roast, tied in twine
	Kosher salt, to taste
	Freshly ground black pepper, to taste
$1/2$	cup red wine
3-4	cups low-sodium beef stock
3-4	cloves garlic, smashed
2	bay leaves
2	tablespoons tomato paste
1	28-ounce can puréed tomatoes
1	large onion, peeled and diced into 1-inch pieces
4	large carrots, peeled and diced into 1-inch pieces
2	pounds Yukon potatoes, diced into 1-inch pieces
1	tablespoon minced fresh thyme
$1/4$	cup minced fresh flat-leaf Italian parsley

1. Preheat oven to 350°F.
2. In a Dutch oven, heat oil over medium-high heat. Season roast on all sides with salt and pepper, place roast in pot, and brown on all sides (including both ends), about 15-20 minutes. Transfer roast to a plate and set aside. Drain grease from pot.
3. Add wine to pot to deglaze, scraping browned bits from bottom. Add roast back to pot along with 3 cups stock, garlic, bay leaves, tomato paste, and puréed tomatoes. Bring to a simmer. Remove from heat, cover, and place pot in oven. Roast for 2 hours, turning roast once halfway during cooking. Remove pot from oven and add onions, carrots, potatoes, thyme, and parsley. If necessary, add more stock to pot so that vegetables are almost covered. Return pot to oven and continue to cook until vegetables are tender, about 45 minutes to 1 hour.
4. Transfer roast to a cutting board and remove twine from around roast. Cut roast into thick slices. Place slices on a serving platter and top with onions, carrots, and potatoes. Using a spoon, skim any fat off surface of cooking liquid and spoon some of sauce over meat and vegetables. Pour remaining sauce into a serving bowl and serve alongside platter.

late summer vegetable pot pies

SERVES 4

When it comes to pot pies, I prefer an individual dish, just for me. I love breaking through the thick, buttery crust, anticipating the taste of that very first molten bite. This is my basic recipe for vegetarian pot pies, but you can easily fold cooked chicken or turkey into the sauce. Substitute the ingredients below with any combination of vegetables you like—almost anything works.

1   bunch curly kale, washed
2   tablespoons unsalted butter
2   large Yukon gold potatoes, diced
1   large onion, diced
1   medium zucchini, diced
    Kosher salt, to taste
    Freshly ground black pepper, to taste
1   clove garlic, finely minced
1/4 cup flour
4   cups low-sodium vegetable stock
1/2 cup heavy cream
1/4 cup chopped fresh flat-leaf Italian parsley
1   egg, beaten and divided
1   package puff pastry, cut into 4 equal pieces, thawed in refrigerator for 1 hour

1. Preheat oven to 375°F.
2. Place 4 12-ounce soufflé dishes on an aluminum foil-lined baking sheet and set aside.
3. Bring a large pot of water to a boil. Grab 1/2 bunch of whole kale by stems and dunk into pot of water, using stems as handles. Swirl around in pot for about 30 seconds. Transfer to a colander and allow to cool. Repeat with remaining kale until all of it is blanched.
4. In a large sauté pan, melt butter over medium heat. Add potatoes, cook until slightly softened, about 5-10 minutes, and season with salt and pepper. Add onions and zucchini and cook until softened, about 5-10 minutes. Add garlic and cook for another 1-2 minutes. Add flour and stir until incorporated into vegetables, about 1 minute. Slowly pour in stock and stir to combine, scraping browned bits from bottom of pan. Cook until sauce is thickened, about 5 minutes. Add cream and cook for another 1-2 minutes.
5. Meanwhile, pat dry kale and remove stems. Chop leaves, fold into thickened sauce along with parsley, and allow to heat through, about 1-2 minutes. Divide mixture equally among prepared soufflé dishes.
6. Brush outside rim of dishes with beaten egg. Place a piece puff pastry over top of each filled dish, allowing to hang over edge about 1 inch. Press down to adhere and trim off any excess. Crimp edges of dough to form a tight edge all around dish. Brush top of pastry with egg and cut a few slits into pastry dough. Repeat with remaining dishes and season top of each with salt and pepper. Bake until tops are golden brown, about 20-25 minutes. Allow to cool slightly before serving.

cook's note: This technique for quickly blanching the kale comes from *New York Times* food writer Melissa Clark and works perfectly as an easy way to blanch the kale before removing it from its stems.

classic shrimp bisque

SERVES 4

I grew up in southern Vermont and spent my childhood hanging out in the kitchen of my parents' restaurant, where one of my jobs always included peeling shrimp. It can be tedious work, but in this instance, the effort is worth it. This is a classic version of bisque, gaining its deep flavor from a broth made of shrimp shells, hints of sherry, and orange zest.

1	pound large shrimp (approximately 20 shrimp), peeled, deveined, and roughly chopped
1	bay leaf
4	strips orange zest
2	cups water
2	cups low-sodium vegetable stock
2	tablespoons extra virgin olive oil
6	tablespoons unsalted butter, divided
2	leeks, white and light green parts, rinsed well and roughly chopped
2	shallots, roughly chopped
	Kosher salt, to taste
	Freshly ground black pepper, to taste
4	cloves garlic, finely chopped
	Pinch of cayenne pepper
1/4	cup plus 2 tablespoons dry sherry
1/4	cup flour
2	cups heavy cream
2	tablespoons tomato paste

1. In a large saucepan, add shrimp shells, bay leaf, orange zest, water, and stock. Cook over medium heat, about 10-15 minutes. Strain and reserve stock.
2. In another large saucepan, heat oil and 2 tablespoons butter over medium heat. Add leeks and shallots, cook until softened, about 7-10 minutes, and season with salt and pepper. Add garlic and cayenne and cook for another 1-2 minutes. Add shrimp and cook, stirring occasionally, until shrimp are cooked through, about 2-3 minutes. Add sherry and cook for another 2-3 minutes. Transfer to a food processor (in batches if necessary) and process a few times until puréed but mixture still has some texture (see cook's note).
3. In same saucepan, melt remaining 4 tablespoons butter. Add flour and cook over medium-low heat for 1 minute, stirring to incorporate flour and scraping browned bits from bottom of pan. Add cream and whisk until mixture thickens, about 1-2 minutes. Add reserved stock and tomato paste and stir to combine. Stir in shrimp mixture from food processor and heat until warmed through, about 10 minutes. Season with salt and pepper and serve warm.

cook's note: I like to keep the texture of the shrimp in this soup, but if you prefer the bisque to be completely smooth, simply purée the mixture to your desired texture.

end-of-the-season tomato risotto

SERVES 4

Though we've come to expect tomatoes all year round at supermarkets, the reality is that this summer crop has a short season. In order to extend the season just a little longer, this recipe uses those less-than-perfect garden tomatoes that are past the point of enjoying sliced with a pinch of salt and pepper. Roasting the tomatoes brings out their sweetness, and a quick purée makes them perfect for risotto. The tomatoes should yield about 1½ cups of purée, but don't worry if you have a little more or less. Simply adjust the amount of cooking liquid by adding more or less stock.

8	medium tomatoes, cored and cut into quarters
1	shallot, chopped
2	cloves garlic, roughly chopped
3	tablespoons extra virgin olive oil, divided
	Kosher salt, to taste
	Freshly ground black pepper, to taste
3	cups low-sodium vegetable stock
1	cup Arborio rice
¼	cup white wine
1	tablespoon unsalted butter
¼	cup freshly grated Parmigiano-Reggiano, or to taste, for serving
¼	cup roughly chopped fresh flat-leaf Italian parsley, for serving

1. Preheat oven to 425°F.
2. Place tomatoes, shallot, and garlic on a rimmed baking sheet. Toss with 2 tablespoons olive oil and season with salt and pepper. Bake until tomatoes are soft and bubbly, about 20 minutes. Allow to cool for 5 minutes.
3. Transfer tomatoes, shallot, garlic, and pan drippings to a food processor and purée until almost smooth (there should be just a bit of texture when finished). Mixture should yield about 1½ cups (see headnote). Set aside.
4. Place stock in a medium saucepan over medium-high heat.
5. Heat remaining 1 tablespoon olive oil in a medium saucepan over medium heat. Add rice and cook for 1-2 minutes.
6. Add wine and cook until evaporated, about 2 minutes. Add puréed tomatoes and ½ cup hot stock and stir. When mixture starts to look creamy and some of stock has been absorbed, add another ½ cup stock, stirring consistently (add each ½ cup of stock before mixture starts to look dry). When rice has absorbed most of liquid, repeat again with another ½ cup stock about 3-5 minutes later. Reduce heat to medium-low. Continue with another ½ cup stock (2 cups total), and continue stirring until rice is tender and creamy, about 20-25 minutes (begin tasting rice after 20 minutes to test for texture). Continue cooking if necessary, adding more stock and stirring as needed.
7. Remove from heat and stir in butter. Transfer to serving bowls and garnish with Parmigiano-Reggiano and parsley. Serve immediately.

sweet potato ravioli salad with greens + walnut oil

SERVES 2-4

Making homemade pasta is one of my favorite things to do in the kitchen, especially when autumn sets in and the temperature begins to drop. In this salad, hints of citrus complement and brighten the sweet potato filling, and the toasted walnuts add a nice crunchy contrast. If you can't find walnut oil, simply use extra virgin olive oil instead. (However, when time is short I reach for my freezer, which always has a stash of locally made Venda ravioli; see page 179.)

Sweet Potato Filling
1   extra large sweet potato
2   teaspoons maple syrup
1/2 teaspoon ground cinnamon
1/4 teaspoon ground nutmeg
    Kosher salt, to taste
    Freshly ground black pepper, to taste

Pasta Dough
1   cup semolina flour, sifted
1   cup all-purpose flour, sifted
3   extra large eggs
1   tablespoon extra virgin olive oil
1   teaspoon water

1   tablespoon extra virgin olive oil
1   medium onion, thinly sliced
1   small clove garlic, finely minced
2   tablespoons white wine
1   bunch kale, stemmed and roughly chopped (or spinach, washed)
1   cup low-sodium vegetable stock
    Zest from 1/2 orange
2   tablespoons walnut oil
1/4 cup chopped walnuts, toasted
    Freshly grated Parmigiano-Reggiano, for serving

1. Preheat oven to 425°F.
2. Line a baking sheet with aluminum foil. Place sweet potato on prepared baking sheet and, using a fork, prick a few holes into top of sweet potato. Bake until tender, about 1 hour. Allow to cool slightly.
3. Meanwhile, make pasta dough. In a medium bowl, combine flours. Transfer to counter and form a well in center of mound, making sure sides are high. Carefully crack eggs into well and add a pinch of salt, oil, and water. Using a fork, slowly break apart eggs. Bring some flour into well, and carefully mix until eggs and flour in well are incorporated. Pull more flour into well, a little at a time, until most of flour has been incorporated and dough has formed. Knead dough with hands for about 5 minutes, adding flour to dough and your hands as necessary (dough should be soft but not sticky when finished). Wrap dough in plastic wrap and refrigerate for 30 minutes.
4. Prepare ravioli filling. Peel and dice cooled sweet potato, transfer to a food processor, and pulse until puréed. Transfer 2 cups to a medium bowl (reserve any extra sweet potato for another use). To bowl, add maple syrup,

cinnamon, and nutmeg, season with salt and pepper, and stir to combine.

5. Cut pasta dough into quarters. Flour one piece and gently stretch it into a slight rectangular shape to get it started through pasta machine. With pasta machine on setting #1, feed floured dough through, guiding dough from underneath (doing so prevents it from getting stuck inside machine). Fold dough into thirds and pass through two more times (folding in thirds each time) on same setting, flouring dough as necessary to prevent it from sticking. Increase to setting #2; fold dough into thirds, and pass through three times on this setting, folding into thirds each time. Increase to setting #3 (do not fold) and pass dough through once. Continue this process until dough is smooth (through setting #6). Place finished sheet of pasta on a floured surface and repeat with remaining quarters of dough (you'll have four long sheets when finished).

6. Place a bit of water in a small bowl and set aside.

7. Using a teaspoon, place 12 small mounds of sweet potato filling down center of one sheet of pasta, spacing out as needed so that your cutter will fit easily around each mound. Using a pastry brush, lightly brush around each mound with water (this will seal dough in next step).

8. Carefully place a second sheet of pasta dough evenly over top. Using a ravioli cutter, cookie cutter, or $2\frac{1}{2}$ inch wide glass, cut out rounds of dough, making 12 ravioli. Use your fingers or a fork to gently press around entire ravioli and seal dough. Dust a baking sheet with a little bit of flour and place ravioli on pan in a single layer. Repeat with remaining sheets of dough and filling, making 24 ravioli total. Set aside 12 ravioli for use in salad.

9. To freeze remaining 12 ravioli, place in a single layer on floured baking sheet and put in freezer until frozen, at least 1 hour. Transfer ravioli to a freezer bag, store in freezer, and save for a later use.

10. Bring a pot of water to boil and add salt. Add 12 fresh ravioli to boiling water and cook until they float to surface, about 4-5 minutes. Remove with a slotted spoon, transfer to a large plate, and set aside.

11. In a large sauté pan, heat olive oil over medium heat. Add onions, cook until softened, 5-10 minutes, and season with salt and pepper. Add garlic and cook for another 1-2 minutes. Add wine to deglaze pan, scraping browned bits from bottom of pan. Add kale and cook until it begins to turn bright green and wilts slightly, about 1-2 minutes. Add stock and cook until kale is wilted, another 5 minutes. Stir in orange zest. Add ravioli to pan (taking care not to break them) and cook until ravioli is just warmed through, about 1-2 minutes.

12. Divide ravioli and kale among serving bowls. Drizzle each with walnut oil and 1 tablespoon walnuts, top with a handful of Parmigiano-Reggiano, season with salt and pepper, and serve.

cook's note: When folding ravioli on settings #1 and #2, it's best to feed the pasta through the machine in the shape of a rectangle. Doing so will ensure the pasta will come out in long, thin sheets when you feed it through on settings #3 to #6.

CHEF RECIPE

pan-roasted duck with toasted farro, kale + rainier cherry mostarda

SERVES 4

From Matthew Varga, Chef, Gracie's, Providence, RI.

Each summer we receive an abundance of Rainier cherries at their peak. In order to showcase their versatility, we incorporate the cherries in different menu selections. Some are sliced for a salad; others are preserved for cheese. One thing is for sure: these sun-kissed jewels are certain to please the palate. The Rainier cherry mostarda used in this recipe will store for a long time if covered in the refrigerator.

Rainier Cherry Mostarda

1/3 cup sugar
1/4 cup good red wine
1 teaspoon mustard seed
   Pinch of kosher salt
   Pinch of freshly ground black pepper
1 pound Rainier cherries, pitted
2 tablespoons hot mustard oil (or mustard powder)

Toasted Farro

3 cups homemade (or low-sodium) chicken stock
1 cup farro
2 tablespoons extra virgin olive oil
1 small white onion, diced
1 clove garlic, chopped
1/2 pound young red Russian kale, stems removed
1 tablespoon chopped fresh flat-leaf Italian parsley
1 teaspoon fresh thyme
2 tablespoons toasted pine nuts, optional

4 duck breasts, trimmed and fat side scored

1. Make mostarda. Combine all ingredients except for cherries and mustard oil (or mustard powder) in a heavy-bottomed saucepan. Bring to a boil then simmer. Reduce liquid to a syrupy consistency, stirring to make sure sugar does not burn. Add cherries and mustard oil and continue cooking until cherries are soft and mixture starts to thicken. Transfer mixture to a shallow, flat pan and place in refrigerator to cool until ready to use.

2. Preheat oven to 400°F.

3. Make farro. In a small saucepan, bring chicken stock to a light simmer. Heat a medium to large sauté pan to medium-high heat. Add farro and toast until fragrant. Add chicken stock, simmer for about 12 minutes or until tender, and season with a pinch of salt and pepper. Drain farro, transfer to a baking sheet, and allow to cool.

4. Wipe same sauté pan clean, and place back over medium-high heat. Add olive oil, onions, and garlic and cook until vegetables are tender, about 3-5 minutes.

5. Add kale and cook until wilted, about 1 minute. Add cooked farro and toss to mix. Cook thoroughly for 2-3 minutes. Add parsley, thyme, and pine nuts (if using), season with salt and pepper, and set aside.

6. Season duck breasts on both sides with salt and pepper. Place duck breasts in a large, oven-safe sauté pan, skin side down, and place pan over medium heat. Allow fat to render out and cook until golden and crisp, about 6-8 minutes. Turn duck breasts over, place pan in oven, and bake for another 2-3 minutes for medium rare. Remove duck breasts from pan and allow to rest for a few minutes before slicing.

7. When ready to serve, divide toasted farro mixture among serving plates. Top each with sliced duck breast, spoon cherry mostarda on top of duck, and serve.

VENDA RAVIOLI

Walk into Venda Ravioli in the historic Federal Hill district in Providence, RI and the first thing you'll notice is the large display case filled with a mouth-watering selection of prepared Italian dishes, meats, and cheeses. Part Italian market, part restaurant, Venda Ravioli has been known as "Rhode Island's Italian Grocery Store" for more than seventy years.

Alan Costantino purchased Venda Ravioli in 1972 and, over the last four decades, the shop has become one of the most well respected Italian food markets in the area. The space, which was designed by Costantino himself, carries a complete selection of Italian specialties, but it's their old-world style pasta that has made Venda Ravioli famous. The ravioli comes in a variety of flavors, including cheese, pumpkin, and lobster—by far the most popular. In addition to the ravioli, however, Venda's display cases also boast a vast assortment of manicotti, tortellini, agnolotti, and angel hair.

Venda Ravioli is a great place to stock up on homemade pasta and sauces, but be sure to bring an appetite, as you'll want to grab a seat at the six-person espresso bar, have lunch inside, or venture across the plaza to their restaurant, Costantino's Ristorante. With such a wide selection of amazing choices to nibble on while you shop, something will most certainly tempt you.

chouriço-stuffed pork loin with garlic mash

SERVES 4-6

This basic stuffing recipe gains a hint of spice and a flavorful bite from ground chouriço. It works perfectly with roast pork and is a satisfying weekend meal or a sophisticated, yet homey, dish when served to company. You can dice leftover pork and stuffing and combine them for a simple weeknight hash, with or without a fried egg on top.

4   pieces of butcher's twine, each cut to about 12 inches in length

Garlic Mash
1   head garlic
1   tablespoon extra virgin olive oil
8   medium Yukon gold potatoes
4   tablespoons unsalted butter
1/2 cup milk (or cream)
    Kosher salt, to taste
    Freshly ground black pepper, to taste

Chouriço Stuffing
1   pound ground chouriço
3   tablespoons extra virgin olive oil, divided
1/2 medium onion, finely diced
2   cloves garlic, finely minced
1/4 cup plain breadcrumbs

1   2-pound boneless pork loin roast
2   cups low-sodium vegetable stock, divided
1   tablespoon unsalted butter

1. Preheat oven to 400°F.
2. Cut off very top of garlic bulb to expose garlic cloves. Place garlic bulb in center of a piece of aluminum foil large enough to cover whole bulb and drizzle with 1 tablespoon olive oil. Wrap tightly, twisting foil at top. Place on a baking sheet and roast until garlic is fragrant and golden in color, about 1 hour. Remove from oven and set aside to cool. When cooled, remove from foil, squeeze garlic into a small bowl, mash well, and set aside.
3. Reduce oven temperature to 350°F.
4. Make stuffing. In a large non-stick pan, cook chouriço over medium heat until golden brown and cooked through. Remove with a slotted spoon, transfer to a small bowl, and set aside. To pan, add 1 tablespoon olive oil over medium heat. Add onion, cook until softened, about 5-10 minutes, and season with salt and pepper. Add garlic and cook for another 1-2 minutes. Transfer onion mixture to bowl of chouriço and mix together. Add breadcrumbs and 1 tablespoon olive oil and mix until combined (mixture will be a bit loose).
5. Remove string from pork loin and discard. Grab your new, cut butcher's twine and have it ready. Place pork loin on a cutting board with fat side facing out on left. Using a sharp knife, carefully slice pork loin, so it opens like a book. (Take care not to cut completely through pork loin.) Cut as deep as you need so that pork loin will open flat. Place a large piece of wax paper over pork loin, and using a mallet or rolling pan, gently pound out pork until it's uniform in thickness, about 1 inch. (This ensures pork loin will cook evenly.) Turn cutting board so that pork loin is lengthwise.

6. Spread stuffing evenly over interior of pork loin, leaving about a ½-inch border on all sides. Gently press stuffing into pork loin, adhering it to pork as best you can. Slowly roll up pork lengthwise, enclosing as much stuffing as you can (some will fall out; that's ok) ending with seam side on bottom. Tie pork at 4 different intervals with your butcher's twine, just tight enough to hold pork and stuffing together. (Stuff in any excess on either end if possible.) Cut off extra twine at knots and season outside of pork with salt and pepper.

7. In a large roasting pan or Dutch oven, heat remaining 1 tablespoon olive oil over medium-high heat. Add pork loin, seam-side down, and sear on all sides until golden brown, about 10-12 minutes.

8. Add 1 cup stock to pan and place in oven. Cook, uncovered, for about 35-45 minutes. The cooked roast should have an interior temperature of 140-145° (be sure to not to hit stuffing when testing temperature).

9. Meanwhile, make garlic mash. Peel and dice potatoes and add to a large stockpot with enough cold water to cover potatoes. Add a pinch of salt and bring to a boil; reduce heat to simmer until potatoes are fork tender, about 30 minutes. Drain potatoes. Pass potatoes through a ricer (in batches) and return potatoes to stockpot. Add 2 tablespoons butter and ¼ cup milk, stir until combined, and season with salt and pepper. Add mashed garlic and mix well. Add more butter or milk, if necessary, to reach desired consistency. Keep pot over low heat while you finish pork loin. Remove pan from oven. Transfer pork to a cutting board and cover loosely with aluminum foil. Allow to rest for 10 minutes.

10. Return pan to stove. Add remaining 1 cup stock and bring to a boil. Reduce heat to low and allow sauce to thicken, about 10 minutes. Stir in butter until melted.

11. Remove twine from pork and discard. Cut pork into slices.

12. Place mashed potatoes on each serving plate and top with 1 or 2 slices of pork. Drizzle sauce over pork and serve warm.

cook's note: I prefer to use a ricer for making mashed potatoes because it makes light, fluffy, lump-free potatoes. If you don't have one, however, just use a potato masher or mash by hand.

roasted cauliflower with parmesan

SERVES 4

For this simple recipe, break the cauliflower into large florets and then cut them into thick slices. The goal is to have as many flat sides as possible so that the cauliflower gets a crisp exterior. Roasting the cauliflower brings out its sweetness, and freshly grated Parmigiano-Reggiano adds a nice salty bite.

1   head cauliflower, stems removed and sliced into thick pieces
2   tablespoons extra virgin olive oil
    Kosher salt, to taste
    Freshly ground black pepper, to taste
2   ounces freshly grated Parmigiano-Reggiano, or to taste

1. Preheat oven to 425°F.
2. Place cauliflower on baking sheet, drizzle with olive oil, and season with salt and pepper. Carefully toss cauliflower on baking sheet, making sure it's well coated with oil. Bake, turning once halfway through, until golden brown, about 20-25 minutes (depending on how thick slices are).
3. Carefully remove baking sheet from oven and sprinkle with enough Parmigiano-Reggiano to lightly coat tops of cauliflower. Place baking sheet back in oven, continue to bake until cheese is melted, about 1-2 minutes, transfer to a serving platter, and serve warm.

cook's note: Leftover cauliflower is delicious reheated and served over a bowl of warm spaghetti.

crispy polenta with sausage ragu

SERVES 4

Here, sliced polenta is pan fried and finished with a thick sausage ragu (though you can substitute ground turkey or beef if you prefer). In order to get a good crust on the polenta, it is important to allow the slices to cook without moving them around in the pan. This is a great dish for company, as you can make the polenta up to a day in advance and finish as your guests are sitting down at the table.

Polenta
- Cooking spray
- 2¼ cups water
- Kosher salt, to taste
- ¾ cup polenta (yellow corn grits)
- Freshly ground black pepper, to taste
- 1 tablespoon heavy cream
- 4 tablespoons freshly grated Parmigiano-Reggiano, divided, plus extra for garnish
- 2 tablespoons extra virgin olive oil

Sausage Ragu
- 1 tablespoon extra virgin olive oil
- 2 spicy (or sweet) Italian sausage links, casings removed
- ½ medium onion, diced
- 2 cloves garlic, minced
- 2 tablespoons red wine
- 3½ cups simple year-round tomato sauce (see page 72)

1. Coat a loaf pan on all sides with cooking spray and set aside.
2. In a medium saucepan, bring water and 1 teaspoon salt to a boil. Slowly whisk in polenta. Reduce heat to simmer and cook until water is evaporated and mixture is thickened and cooked slightly, about 5 minutes, whisking constantly. Season with pepper. Stir in cream and 2 tablespoons Parmigiano-Reggiano. Transfer polenta to prepared loaf pan and smooth out top so mixture is evenly distributed in pan. Cover and refrigerate for at least 2 hours, or overnight.
3. Pour off any liquid that has accumulated on top of polenta. Running a knife along inside of loaf pan, loosen polenta. Place a cutting board on top of loaf pan and gently flip pan over. Cut polenta in half; then cut each half on a diagonal into 2 equal triangles, making 4 equal triangles.
4. Make ragu. In a medium sauté pan, heat 1 tablespoon olive oil over medium-high heat. Add sausage and cook until browned and cooked through, about 7-10 minutes, breaking up sausage into smaller bite-size pieces as it cooks. Using a slotted spoon, transfer sausage to a plate lined with paper towels and set aside. Pour off all but 1 tablespoon oil and add onions. Cook until softened, about 5-7 minutes, and season with salt and pepper. Add garlic and cook for another 1-2 minutes. Deglaze pan with wine, scraping browned bits from bottom of pan. Add tomato sauce to pan and stir to combine. Add sausage back to pan along with remaining 2 tablespoons Parmigiano-Reggiano and cook sauce over low heat until warmed through.
5. Meanwhile, in a large non-stick pan, heat remaining 2 tablespoons olive oil over medium-high heat. Fry polenta until golden brown and a crust has formed, about 5 minutes (if they resist, they aren't ready to flip). Carefully turn polenta over and continue to cook for another 5 minutes.
6. Place sausage ragu in center of a serving platter, place polenta pieces on top, followed by some additional Parmigiano-Reggiano, and serve immediately.

roasted garlic bread with fresh herbs

SERVES 4-6

There was a little Italian restaurant down the street from where I grew up that made the best garlic bread. They'd serve it, all bubbly and warm, as soon as you sat down. While there are countless recipes for garlic bread, this one starts with roasted garlic, which is milder, and finishes beautifully with fresh herbs and Parmigiano-Reggiano.

1   head garlic
3   tablespoons extra virgin olive oil, divided
4   tablespoons unsalted butter, at room
    temperature
    Kosher salt, to taste
    Freshly ground black pepper, to taste
1   tablespoon finely minced fresh flat-leaf Italian
    parsley
1   tablespoon finely minced fresh oregano
1   loaf ciabatta (or Italian bread)
2   tablespoons freshly grated Parmigiano-
    Reggiano

1. Preheat oven to 400°F.
2. Cut off very top of garlic bulb to expose garlic cloves. Place garlic bulb in center of a piece of aluminum foil large enough to cover whole bulb and drizzle with 1 tablespoon olive oil. Wrap tightly, twisting foil at top. Place on a baking sheet and roast until garlic is fragrant and golden in color, about 1 hour. Remove from oven and set aside to cool. When cooled, remove from foil, squeeze garlic into a small bowl, mash well, and set aside.
3. Reduce oven to 350°F.
4. To bowl of garlic, add butter and season with salt and pepper. Add parsley and oregano and combine until garlic and spices are evenly distributed through butter mixture.
5. Slice ciabatta bread in half lengthwise and spread butter mixture on both cut sides of bread. Drizzle remaining 2 tablespoons oil evenly over top of each half. Put halves together and wrap bread in aluminum foil. Place bread in oven and bake for 5 minutes. Carefully open foil and separate bread halves, placing butter sides up. Scatter Parmigiano-Reggiano over top of each half and continue baking on foil for an additional 5 minutes, until cheese is melted and bread is crispy.

6. Turn oven to broil and cook until golden brown around edges of bread, about 30 seconds to 2 minutes. Cut into pieces and serve warm.

cook's note: To save time, you can roast the garlic up to 2 days ahead of when you will need it. If doing so, roast the garlic as noted above and allow it to cool to room temperature. Squeeze out cloves into a bowl, cover with plastic wrap, and refrigerate until ready to use.

CHEF RECIPE

macaroni with heirloom tomato sauce + fresh chevre

SERVES 4-6

From Matthew Jennings, Chef/Owner, Farmstead/La Laiterie, Providence, RI.

This version of mac and cheese is inspired by the late growing season—when heirloom tomatoes are at their best! The tangy goat cheese does a nice job complementing the savory macaroni preparation and the fruity tomato sauce.

2³/₄ pounds heirloom tomatoes (with juice), chopped
2   tablespoons extra virgin olive oil, divided, plus extra for greasing
2   large garlic cloves, minced
¹/₈ teaspoon sugar
    Kosher salt, to taste
2   fresh basil sprigs (or 1 teaspoon chopped fresh oregano)
    Freshly ground black pepper, to taste
4   ounces soft, mild goat cheese
¹/₂ cup freshly grated Parmesan
1   pound of small pasta, penne or macaroni
¹/₂ cup breadcrumbs

1. Bring a large pot of water to a boil.
2. Meanwhile, make tomato sauce. Pulse chopped tomatoes in a food processor until puréed, and set aside. In a large, non-stick pan (or saucepan), heat 1 tablespoon of olive oil over medium heat. Add garlic and cook, stirring, until it begins to smell fragrant, about 30 seconds to 1 minute. Add tomatoes and their juice, sugar, a pinch of salt, and basil (or oregano). Stir and increase heat. When tomatoes begin to bubble, lower heat to medium and cook, stirring often, until thick and fragrant, about 15-20 minutes. Remove basil or oregano sprigs, wipe any sauce adhering to them back into pan, and season sauce with pepper. Stir in goat and Parmesan cheeses until combined. Taste and adjust seasonings.
3. Preheat oven to 350°F.
4. Coat a 2-quart baking dish or gratin dish with olive oil and set aside.
5. When water comes to a boil, add a tablespoon of salt. Add pasta and cook for 1-2 minutes less than instructions on package indicate (pasta should be a little undercooked as it will finish cooking while it bakes in oven). Drain pasta and transfer to a large bowl. Add tomato-goat cheese sauce and stir together until pasta is thoroughly coated. Transfer to prepared baking dish.
6. Toss breadcrumbs with remaining 1 tablespoon of olive oil and sprinkle over top of pasta. Bake until casserole bubbles and breadcrumbs are lightly browned, about 30 minutes. Let stand for 5-10 minutes before serving.

advance preparation: You can make the tomato sauce up to 3 days ahead and keep it in the refrigerator. Reheat and stir in the cheese just before tossing with the pasta. The assembled macaroni will keep for several hours outside of the refrigerator and can be covered and refrigerated for up to 3 days before baking.

NEW RIVERS

Bruce Tillinghast and his late wife, Pat, founded New Rivers in 1990. Situated in the original 1793 warehouse built for iron merchants Congdon and Carpenter, the restaurant's building maintains its historic charm—from the original wide plank floors to the bar made from reclaimed timber to the façade, which was designed to replicate the original storefronts of almost a century ago.

New Rivers, which is named after the river rerouting project that jumpstarted Providence's renaissance, continues to be a forerunner in cooking with locally sourced food thanks in large part to Beau Vestal, the current owner and chef. In the spring of 2012, Beau, the restaurant's longtime executive chef, and his wife Elizabeth purchased New Rivers from Bruce Tillinghast.

During his years at New Rivers, Beau has developed great relationships with Rhode Island and New England's best farmers and producers. These relationships allow him to source product that meet the restaurant's exacting needs; at the same time, New Rivers is able to support the people who work so hard to craft these products.

New Rivers is known for their commitment to hand making as much as they can from scratch. From artisanal bread to pasta to cured meats and charcuterie, Beau believes the best and most honest foods are made within the walls of his restaurant. You can taste it in every bite.

crispy chicken with parsley pesto

SERVES 4

Tucking homemade pesto under the skin of a roasted chicken breast is a beautiful and flavorful way to dress up what could be an otherwise ordinary meal. Prying the skin away from the chicken takes practice, but it's not hard. Just go slowly and try not to tear the skin. If the skin tears, carefully fold it back in place to cover the pesto when you're done.

Parsley Pesto
1   cup packed fresh flat-leaf Italian parsley, washed and dried
1   clove garlic, roughly chopped
     Kosher salt, to taste
     Freshly ground black pepper, to taste
1/4   cup freshly grated Parmigiano-Reggiano
3   tablespoons extra virgin olive oil, plus extra for drizzling

4   bone-in breasts of chicken with skin on

1. Preheat oven to 425°F.
2. Make pesto. In a food processor, combine parsley, garlic, salt, pepper, and Parmigiano-Reggiano. With motor running, slowly stream in olive oil, process until smooth, and set aside.
3. Place chicken breasts on a baking sheet, skin-side up. Separate skin from chicken breast by carefully placing one finger under skin, gently prying it from chicken breast.
4. Using a teaspoon, carefully place some pesto under skin of one chicken breast, as far back as you can. Working your way forward, spread pesto evenly over chicken breast and gently pat skin back in place. Repeat procedure with remaining chicken. Drizzle top of each with a bit of olive oil and season with salt and pepper.
5. Roast until chicken is cooked through and skin is crispy, about 30-35 minutes. If skin isn't as crispy as you'd like it to be, place under broiler for 1-2 minutes. Allow to cool slightly before serving. Transfer chicken breasts to a serving platter and serve warm.

cook's note: With or without the pesto, roasting is my favorite way to cook chicken. Roasting chicken with the bone in and skin on keeps the breasts moist. Once cooked, you can shred the chicken and stir it into soups and stews or use it for chicken salad.

CHEF RECIPE

jalapeño + cheddar cornbread with cranberry butter

MAKES 1 LOAF

From Bob Dillon, Founding Owner/Chef of the Little Red Smokehouse, Carver, MA.

My mom was the inspiration for this recipe. We were a family of modest means and my mom would always figure out ways to make the ordinary extraordinary. My brother and I would wake up to warm cornbread most mornings. She would take a peek in the fridge and incorporate leftovers from dinner into the cornbread: cheese, sausage, taco meat, vegetables—whatever was on hand to make the cornbread more like a meal rather than just a baked good. She said that a good education started with a full tummy, and we were lucky to fill ours with her delicious—and creative—cornbread.

Cranberry Butter
1   stick lightly salted butter, at room temperature
1/2   cup minced dried cranberries
2   tablespoons honey

Cornbread
  Cooking spray
1   stick lightly salted butter
2/3   cup sugar
2   large eggs
1/2   cup buttermilk
1/2   cup creamed corn
1/2   teaspoon baking soda
1   cup cornmeal
1   cup flour
1/2   teaspoon kosher salt
1   cup shredded sharp white cheddar
1/2   cup finely diced jalapeño peppers (about 4 medium sized peppers)

1. Make cranberry butter. Using electric mixer, cream 1 stick butter until light and fluffy. Add minced dried cranberries and mix until combined. Add honey and mix until incorporated. Transfer to a serving bowl, cover with plastic wrap and refrigerate until ready to use.
2. In a small saucepan, melt remaining stick of butter. Allow to cool to room temperature.
3. Preheat oven to 325°F.
4. Coat a loaf pan on bottom and all sides with cooking spray and set aside.
5. In a medium bowl, combine melted butter, sugar, eggs, buttermilk, and creamed corn.
6. In another medium bowl, combine cornmeal, flour, baking soda, and salt. Stir in wet ingredients until just incorporated. Stir in cheddar and jalapeño peppers. Transfer mixture to prepared loaf pan and bake for 45-50 minutes, or until toothpick inserted into center comes out clean (cook an additional 5-10 minutes if necessary). Serve warm cornbread with cranberry butter.

    cook's note: If you prefer a basic cornbread, simply omit the cheddar and jalapeño peppers.

LITTLE RED SMOKEHOUSE

Located in an unassuming strip mall on South Main Street in Carver, the Little Red Smokehouse makes up for the lackluster exterior the minute you walk in the door. But while the rustic, country kitsch interior is fun, it's the food that will keep you coming back.

Inspired by the restaurant's location in "cranberry country," the menu has an extensive offering of cranberry-inspired dishes, the best of which (in my opinion) are the smoked cranberry wings. Perfectly smoked and deep-fried chicken wings are finished in a homemade cranberry BBQ sauce, making for a basket of finger-licking wings like no other. As with all BBQ, a side of cornbread is a must. The one from the Little Red Smokehouse is as good as any you'll find in the South, but it's the side of cranberry honey butter that will do you in.

Carnivores may gravitate toward the traditional brisket or ribs, but no visit would be complete without a bowl of their chili, winner of the 2012, 2011, and 2007 MVY Radio Big Chili Contest. It's thick and hearty, packed with a generous amount of meat and just the right amount of smokiness to blend it all together in one perfect bowl.

chicken madeira with creamy mashed potatoes

SERVES 4

Madeira is a fortified Portuguese wine made in the Madeira Islands, and it is available in both dry and sweet varieties. For this classic dish I use sweet Madeira, as it gives the dish its distinctive flavor.

Creamy Mashed Potatoes

4	medium potatoes, peeled and diced
2-4	tablespoons unsalted butter
	Kosher salt, to taste
	Freshly ground black pepper, to taste
$1/2$	cup milk (or cream)

4	boneless, skinless chicken breasts
2	tablespoons extra virgin olive oil
3	tablespoons unsalted butter, divided
2	cups fresh sliced button mushrooms (about 12)
2	cups sweet Madeira wine
2-3	cups low-sodium beef stock
1	tablespoon finely minced fresh thyme, or to taste

1. Place potatoes in a medium saucepan and add salt. Cover with cold water and bring to a boil over medium-high heat. Cook until potatoes are fork tender, about 20-25 minutes.

2. Drain potatoes and return to pan. Place pan on burner but do not turn it on, as residual heat from burner will help draw out any remaining moisture from potatoes. Allow potatoes to sit for 1-2 minutes. Pass potatoes through ricer (in batches), transferring potatoes into another medium saucepan (or use a hand mixer or masher in pan). Add 2 tablespoons butter and season with salt and pepper. Add in $1/4$ cup milk (or cream) and whip until light and creamy. Add in more butter, milk, or cream as desired. Cover pan and return to stove over low heat to keep potatoes warm.

3. Place one piece of chicken between 2 sheets of parchment paper. Using a mallet or rolling pin, gently pound chicken until about $1/4$-inch thick. Transfer chicken to a plate and repeat with other pieces of chicken. Season both sides of each piece with salt and pepper and set aside.

4. Heat olive oil in a large non-stick sauté pan over medium-high heat. Cook chicken until golden brown, about 4-5 minutes a side (do this in batches if your pan will not hold all of chicken at once). Transfer to a plate and tent with aluminum foil.

5. To same pan, add 2 tablespoons butter over medium heat. Add mushrooms, cook until softened, 2-3 minutes, and season with a pinch of salt and pepper. Remove pan from heat and slowly add in wine. Return pan to heat and deglaze pan, scraping browned bits from bottom of pan. Add $2^1/2$ cups of stock and bring sauce to a boil; reduce heat to low and cook until sauce has thickened slightly, about 10-15 minutes.

6. Return chicken to sauce and add thyme and remaining 1 tablespoon butter. Cook until chicken is warmed through, about 5-10 minutes. Add in a bit more stock if sauce gets too thick. Spoon potatoes onto serving plates, top each with a piece of chicken and some of sauce, and serve warm.

applewood smoked bacon + onion crostata

SERVES 6-8

This rustic tart's free-form style makes it homey, easy to assemble, and very forgiving. If you can't find Applewood smoked bacon, simply substitute with a thick-cut bacon.

Dough

1¼ cups flour, plus extra for dusting
1   teaspoon sugar
½   teaspoon kosher salt
1   stick unsalted butter, chilled and cut into small cubes
4   tablespoons ice water

4   slices Applewood smoked bacon, chopped
1   tablespoon unsalted butter
2   large Vidalia onions, thinly sliced
    Freshly ground black pepper, to taste
1   tablespoon chopped fresh thyme, plus extra for garnish
2   tablespoons low-sodium beef stock
2   cups grated sharp cheddar cheese
1   large egg
    Cornmeal, for dusting
2   tablespoons freshly grated Parmigiano-Reggiano

1. Make dough. In a food processor, combine flour, sugar, and salt. Add butter and process until mixture becomes coarse crumbs, about 10 seconds. With machine running, add ice water, one tablespoon at a time, in a slow, steady stream through feed tube. Pulse until dough holds together, no more than 30 seconds. Dough should not be wet or sticky. Test finished dough by squeezing a small amount of dough together to see if it holds its shape. If still crumbly, add more ice water, 1 tablespoon at a time.
2. Wrap dough in plastic and flatten into a disc. Refrigerate for about 1 hour.
3. In a large sauté pan, add bacon and cook over medium heat until nicely browned. Remove with a slotted spoon, transfer to a plate lined with paper towels, and set aside. Pour off and discard all but 1 tablespoon of grease from pan.
4. Place a pizza stone on middle rack in oven and preheat oven to 375°F.
5. Place sauté pan back on heat and add butter to remaining bacon fat. When melted, add onions and season with salt and pepper. Cook onions until softened and golden brown, about 20 minutes. Add thyme and cook for another 1-2 minutes.
6. Add stock to pan to deglaze, scraping browned bits from bottom of pan. Allow to cook until stock is evaporated. Remove pan from heat.
7. Lightly flour a pizza peel (or cutting board) and set aside.
8. Remove dough from refrigerator and unwrap. On a lightly floured surface, gently roll dough with a floured rolling pin into a large circle, about ¼-inch thick. Transfer dough to pizza peel.
9. Scatter cheddar cheese on dough, leaving about a 1-inch border around outside edge. Scatter onions and bacon evenly over cheese. Starting at end nearest you, fold up 1-inch border of pastry by lifting dough slightly over filling. Continue doing this around entire crostata, pleating dough as you go to secure it together. (Pleating dough will prevent filling from oozing out during baking.) Center of filling will still be exposed when you're finished; you should have an enclosed, 1-inch border around entire crostata.
10. In a small bowl, beat egg with 1 tablespoon water. Brush outside edge of dough with egg wash and season dough with salt and pepper.
11. Carefully pull rack out from oven and dust a thin layer of cornmeal onto hot pizza stone (this will prevent crostata from sticking to stone). Transfer crostata to pizza stone and bake until crust is golden brown, about 30-35 minutes. Remove crostata from oven and sprinkle Parmigiano-Reggiano cheese over top, followed by fresh thyme for garnish. Allow to cool for 5-10 minutes before slicing.

homemade ricotta gnocchi

SERVES 4

Gnocchi are soft dumplings typically made from potatoes or ricotta cheese. People are often surprised by how easy to make and versatile gnocchi are. Once you have the basic recipe down, you can modify the flavor, as well as the sauce in which they are served, any way you like. Switch out the fresh lemon juice specified here for my simple year-round tomato sauce (see page 72), or change the flavor of the gnocchi altogether by adding freshly minced herbs or pesto to the dough. You can serve these gnocchi right after they boil, but in this recipe I sear them after they have cooked, giving the gnocchi a satisfying, crusty exterior.

1¼ cups flour, plus extra for dusting
1   16-ounce container whole-milk ricotta
¼   cup freshly grated Parmigiano-Reggiano,
      plus extra for garnish
¼   cup finely minced fresh flat-leaf Italian parsley,
      divided
2   large eggs, beaten
      Kosher salt, to taste
      Freshly ground black pepper, to taste
2   tablespoons unsalted butter
      Zest from 1 lemon
      Juice from 1-2 lemons

1. Lightly dust a large baking sheet with a thin layer of flour and set aside.
2. Bring a large pot of water to a boil.
3. Drain off any excess liquid from ricotta and add ricotta to a large bowl. Lightly whisk ricotta for about 10 seconds (it should be smooth, creamy, and free of visible curds when finished). Stir in Parmigiano-Reggiano, 2 tablespoons parsley, and eggs and season with salt and pepper. Mix until everything is incorporated. Start adding flour, ¼ cup at a time, mixing well after each addition. Continue adding flour until you've added in 1¼ cups total. Dough should come away from edge of bowl and should be soft and slightly moist when finished. If it is too wet, add more flour, 1 tablespoon at a time, as necessary.
4. When water boils, add a large pinch of salt. To test dough, form a small ball of dough and drop into boiling water. (If dough stays together as it cooks, it is ready. If it falls apart, work in more flour.)
5. Lightly flour a large work surface and remove dough from bowl. Dust your hands with flour (keep them floured until all of dough is rolled and cut). Divide dough into 4 equal parts. Roll out each section into a 1-inch thick rope. Lightly flour a sharp knife and cut each rope into 1-inch pieces. Transfer cut gnocchi to prepared floured baking sheet, making sure to keep cut gnocchi in one layer.
6. Reduce boiling water to medium-high and drop ½ of gnocchi into water (cook in batches to avoid overcrowding pot). Stir water so that gnocchi don't stick together as they cook. Cook until they float to top of water, about 2-3 minutes. Remove with a slotted spoon and place on a large plate in a single layer. Repeat this cooking process for remaining gnocchi.
7. In a large non-stick pan, melt butter over medium-high heat. Add gnocchi (or do this in batches if they all won't fit in one layer in your pan) and allow to cook, without stirring, for about 4-5 minutes. Once a golden brown crust has formed on bottom of gnocchi, turn them and cook until crust has formed on other side, about another 2-3 minutes.
8. Divide gnocchi among serving bowls and top each with equal amounts of lemon zest and remaining 2 tablespoons parsley. Squeeze a generous amount of lemon juice over top of each serving, followed by a dusting of Parmigiano-Reggiano. Season with salt and pepper and serve warm.

cook's note: When I make ricotta gnocchi, I always use Narragansett Creamery Renaissance Ricotta, though any whole-milk ricotta will suffice. Keep in mind that the amount of flour you'll need to form the dough depends on how much moisture is in your ricotta, so be sure to drain off the excess before you begin. You may also want to make more than one batch at a time. To do so, simply spread extra gnocchi on a floured baking sheet and place them in the freezer. Once they're frozen, transfer to a freezer bag and store in freezer until ready to use.

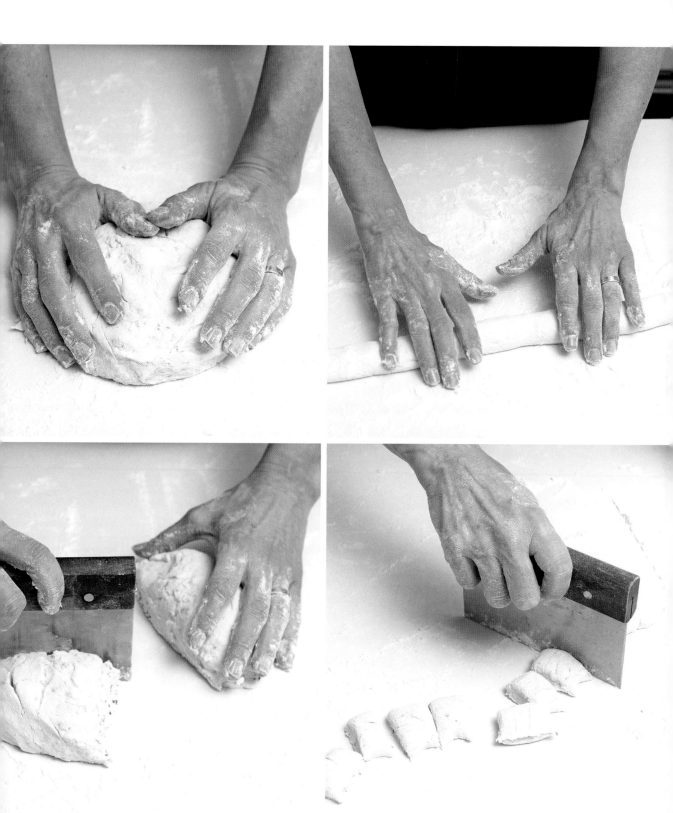

CHEF RECIPE

macomber turnip hash with shredded pork + eggs

SERVES 4-6

From Aaron DeRego, Chef/Co-Owner, The Back Eddy, Westport, MA

This dish uses the Macomber turnip, or Westport White Turnip, which is available from late September through January throughout the South Coast. The pulled pork recipe is similar to the one developed by Chris Schlesinger, one of the original owners of The Back Eddy (and former owner of the East Coast Grill in Cambridge).

Shredded Pork
3   tablespoons paprika
2   tablespoons packed light brown sugar
1   tablespoon kosher salt
1   tablespoon dry mustard
1   tablespoon chile pepper
1   tablespoon ground cumin
1   teaspoon cayenne pepper
1   teaspoon freshly ground black pepper
1   4-pound pork roast (shoulder or butt)

Macomber Turnip Hash
2   medium Macomber turnips, peeled and diced
3   carrots, peeled and diced
2   tablespoons extra virgin olive oil
1   medium red onion, diced
1   bulb fresh fennel, diced
1   red pepper, seeded and diced
    Kosher salt, to taste
    Freshly ground black pepper, to taste
1/4 cup fresh herbs (any combination of sage, rosemary, or oregano), chopped

4   large eggs (poached, fried, or over easy), for serving

1. In a medium bowl, combine paprika, brown sugar, salt, dry mustard, chile pepper, cumin, cayenne, and black pepper. Rub generously all over pork, inside and out, until nicely coated. Cover with plastic wrap and allow to marinate in refrigerator overnight.

2. Preheat oven to 325°F.

3. Line a roasting pan with aluminum foil and place a wire rack in pan. Place pork on rack and cover with parchment paper. Cover entire pan with aluminum foil and cook, covered, for 2^1/$_2$ hours. Remove parchment paper and aluminum foil and continue cooking for another 15-20 minutes (when pork can easily be shredded with a fork, it's done).

4. Remove pork from oven and transfer to a cutting board. Allow to cool until you can touch it, about 5 minutes. While pork is still warm, pull meat apart, shredding with two forks. Transfer shredded pork to a bowl and set aside.

5. Make hash. In medium saucepan, bring 2 quarts of lightly salted water to boil. Add turnips and carrots and cook until vegetables are tender, about 5 minutes. Remove vegetables with a slotted spoon and set aside.

6. In a large skillet, heat olive oil over medium-high heat until hot but not smoking. Add drained turnips and carrots to pan in a single layer covering bottom of pan. Cook until browned on one side before turning, about 4-5 minutes. Once you start turning, add onions, fennel, and red pepper and season with salt and pepper. Continue cooking until vegetables are just tender and golden brown, about 4-5 minutes. Do not overcook. Stir in herbs just before serving.

7. Divide hash among serving bowls, top with some shredded pork, finish with desired style of egg, and serve warm.

THE MACOMBER TURNIP

The Macomber turnip is such an illustrious vegetable that it even has its own historic marker. Located on Main Street in Westport, RI, the turnip's plaque tells the story of this vegetable, from its beginning as a seed to its current status as a symbol for the town in which it was born.

As the legend goes, the turnip was created back in 1876, when brothers and local farmers Adin and Elihu Macomber planted rutabaga seeds (a crossbreed of a cabbage and turnip) next to their radishes as a cross-pollination experiment. The result is the now-famous turnip—at least throughout Southeastern Massachusetts. Only a few people in the area produce the Macomber turnip, and it's pretty scarce anywhere outside the region, so when you see this wonderfully versatile vegetable, grab it.These turnips have a pale, white inner flesh and, when cooked, a lovely sweetness. It's also high in fiber, calcium, potassium, and low in calories.

THE BACK EDDY

The Back Eddy is a popular restaurant along the coast, and for good reason. Its laid-back atmosphere and great food attract people from all over the area. The back deck is a destination in and of itself, a perfect place to unwind with a cocktail and watch a killer sunset over the Westport River.

pick-your-own strawberry milkshakes

sweets

pick-your-own strawberry milkshakes

red wine truffles

vanilla panna cotta with berries, shortbread crumble + lemon granita

ice cream with spanish olive oil

almond citrus biscotti

afternoon applesauce cake with spiced whipped cream

creamy coffee milk pudding

cranberry applesauce

sunset ice cream cake

No matter the season, something sweet at the end of a meal is always a welcome conclusion. In the summer, dessert can be as a simple as bowl of fresh berries or a scoop of homemade ice cream. But in the cooler months, freshly baked cakes and treats fill the house with their intoxicating aroma. These recipes celebrate the sweet flavors of New England and are perfect to share with friends at a casual afternoon get-together or for easy entertaining.

pick-your-own strawberry milkshakes

SERVES 2

I was always a chocolate milkshake kind of a girl—
vanilla or strawberry never stood a chance. But
once I made my first milkshake with freshly picked
strawberries, there was no going back. Plump and
juicy strawberries are the perfect option for a summertime treat, and nothing is better than making
your own homemade version after a day of berry-
picking. I prefer my milkshakes thick (so thick that
you can barely drink them through the straw). If you
want yours a bit thinner, add more milk until you
reach the consistency you prefer.

1   pint fresh strawberries, hulled and sliced
1½ pints strawberry ice cream
½   cup milk, or to taste
1   teaspoon vanilla extract

1. In a blender, combine strawberries, ice
   cream, ½ cup milk, and vanilla and blend
   until smooth. Add in more milk if a thinner
   consistency is desired.
2. Divide between two large glasses and serve.

red wine truffles

MAKES APPROXIMATELY 16-18 TRUFFLES

Because chocolate truffles are often made entirely
with bittersweet chocolate, they are never quite
sweet enough for me. For a better balance, I make
these truffles with equal parts bittersweet and semisweet chocolate and lace them with the deep, rich
flavor of Jester wine from Travessia Urban Winery
in New Bedford, MA. Jester is a blend of California
zinfandel, cabernet sauvignon, syrah, and petite
sirah and has a wonderful, earthy flavor that pairs
beautifully with chocolate. Making truffles is easy,
but it's important to finely chop the chocolate, which
will allow it to melt easily.

4   ounces bittersweet chocolate
4   ounces semisweet chocolate
½   cup heavy cream
2   tablespoons unsalted butter
2   tablespoons Jester, or a similar red wine
     Fleur de sel (or sea salt), to taste

1. Chop chocolate as finely as you can with a sharp
   knife. Place chocolate in a heat-proof bowl and
   set aside.
2. Heat cream in a small saucepan until it just boils
   (small bubbles should form on outside of pan).
   Add butter and cook until it melts. Pour over
   chocolate and, using a heat-proof spatula, slowly
   stir until chocolate is completely melted. Stir in
   wine. Refrigerate mixture for at least 2 hours.
3. Line a baking sheet (or large plate) with parchment paper. Using a teaspoon, form balls of
   chocolate that are about 1 inch in size. Using
   your hands, roll into smooth, round balls and place
   on prepared baking sheet (wet your hands if
   necessary to prevent chocolate from sticking).
   Dust tops of each truffles with a little sea salt.
   Refrigerate until firm, about 30 minutes, and serve
   chilled.

cook's note: I prefer to use Ghirardelli brand
chocolate (60% bittersweet), but any good quality
chocolate will work. If the chocolate doesn't completely melt after you add the cream, simply place
the bowl in the microwave for a few seconds to
finish it.

travessia urban winery, new bedford, ma

Travessia, a small urban winery in the heart of downtown New Bedford, MA, focuses on making high quality wines with Massachusetts-grown grapes. Marco Montez started Travessia, which translates from Portuguese as "a passage or journey," in 2008.

Marco comes from a family of winemakers from the Trás-os-Montes region of Portugal. When he was six years old, his parents bought a piece of land overlooking the tiny village of Loivos, where his mother, grandmother, and great-grandmother were all born. They planted a vineyard, along with one hundred olive trees, and Marco began his love of winemaking by helping his family with the grape harvest. "In those days, everyone made wine and had their own vineyard," Marco says. "Everyone had barrels of wine in their basements."

But when Marco was about twelve, things got tough for his family, and they had to move out of the village, leaving their beloved vineyard behind.

Shortly thereafter, Marco came to New Bedford to live with family. After years of study and a long professional career as an electrical engineer, he decided to return to his passion for wine. His analytical mind got to wondering about the actual process of winemaking and the logistics of the fermentation process, parts of the process he had never thought of before. Once he dove back into winemaking, he fell in love all over again, and Travessia was born.

Travessia produces white, red, and rosé wines. Marco's philosophy is to "make the best possible wine you can with the fruit that you have," and that's just what he does. He uses grapes for his whites from other local wineries (Westport Rivers and Running Brook) and red grapes from California and Washington State.

But relying on other wineries for grapes comes with a set of challenges. Other vineyards can only sell him what they don't need. When they have a bad year, there are fewer available grapes. Buying grapes from others means you need all the money upfront. With product tied up in barrels for at least nine months, paying for your supplies before you can sell your finished product makes cash flow an issue. "In a very short period of time, I've learned that winemaking presents tremendous risks and enormous challenges," says Marco. "It's farming, chemistry, marketing, and sales." But he's passionate about what he does and it shows. For Marco, it's always quality over quantity. He enjoys the freedom of developing and creating his own varietals and working with what the elements have given them. He believes in the wine he is making and is finding his own little niche in the business.

Business is going well and Marco has his eyes on the future. Three years ago he and his father went back to their land in Portugal, cleared it out, and started another vineyard from scratch. The soil there is rocky but rich in minerals, making it great for their vines. The region's hot days and cool nights help preserve the acidity in the grapes and keep them balanced. So far Marco and his father have planted about 16,000 vines on the original property, as well as on two adjacent pieces of land they purchased. The wines from the Portuguese vineyard will be very different from the varietals Marco is currently making at Travessia. They are a more traditional, old-world style, giving Marco a chance to get back to his roots.

CHEF RECIPE

vanilla panna cotta with berries, shortbread crumble + lemon granita

SERVES 4

From Champe Speidel, Chef/Owner, Persimmon, Bristol RI, and Persimmon Provisions, Barrington, RI

This is one of my favorite summer desserts. It's straightforward and can be prepared in advance. While rich, the yogurt and lemon granita add a lovely acidity to the panna cotta. The ginger liquor is optional, but provides a great depth of flavor.

Panna Cotta
1/2 cup heavy cream
1   vanilla bean, split and scraped
1/2 cup sugar
1   cup Narragansett Creamery whole milk yogurt
1/2 cup mascarpone cheese
2 1/2 sheets of silver gelatin

Shortbread
1   cup unsalted butter (2 sticks)
1/2 cup sugar
1   teaspoon vanilla extract
     Pinch of salt
3   cups flour

Lemon Granita
1/4 cup sugar
1/4 cup cold water
1   cup lemon juice
1   tablespoon minced lemon zest

4   cups ripe mixed berries
2   tablespoons ginger liquor (Domaine Canton)
1   tablespoon sugar
     Fresh mint or lemon balm, for garnish, optional

1. Make panna cotta. In a medium saucepan, bring cream, vanilla, and sugar to a boil. Remove from heat and allow to infuse for at least 1 hour.
2. In a large mixing bowl, combine yogurt and mascarpone cheese.
3. Soften gelatin sheets in cold water until pliable, about 2 minutes. Wring out excess water and add to cream mixture. Combine cream with yogurt and mascarpone mixture and stir until smooth. Strain through a fine chinois into a pourable container. Fill 4 shallow serving bowls (no more than 4 ounces in each), leaving at least 1 inch from top of each bowl. Allow panna cotta to set in refrigerator for at least 3 hours.
4. Make shortbread. Preheat oven to 350°F. Line a baking sheet with a silicone baking sheet (or grease a piece of parchment paper) and set aside.
5. In a stand mixer, cream butter and sugar. Add vanilla and salt and fold in flour (do not overmix). Combine into a ball and wrap in plastic. Allow dough to rest and chill in refrigerator for at least 30 minutes.
6. Remove dough and roll out onto a lightly floured surface, until about 1/4-inch thick. Transfer dough to baking sheet. Using a fork, randomly poke holes throughout surface of dough to retard rising. Bake, rotating every 7 minutes, until shortbread is evenly golden brown. Allow shortbread to cool, then break into a crumble.
7. Make lemon granita. First, make simple syrup. In a small saucepan, add sugar and water and bring to a boil. Stir until sugar dissolves. Cover and steep for 10-15 minutes. Remove from heat and cool completely.
8. Combine 1 ounce simple syrup, lemon juice, and lemon zest in a shallow pan. Place in freezer until it begins to solidify. Scrape semi-frozen mixture with a fork to create small, frozen granules. Place pan back in freezer and repeat process until granita is frozen and consistent in size, at least 2 hours or overnight. Keep frozen until ready to use.
9. When ready to serve, gently toss berries, liquor, and sugar together in a large bowl.
10. Remove panna cotta from refrigerator. Sprinkle each with shortbread crumble (reserve extra for later use). Add mixed berries to top, and finish with a bit of lemon granita. Garnish with mint or lemon balm (if using) and serve.

ACUSHNET CREAMERY

There is nothing more quintessentially New England than a few scoops of ice cream on a warm summer evening. Travel from Maine to Connecticut, though, and you'll come across countless ice cream types, recipes, and traditions. Here on the South Coast of Massachusetts and in Rhode Island, an ice cream shop is largely known as a "creamery" and milkshakes are usually called a "cabinet." There are renowned creameries all over the region, but one of my local favorites, Acushnet Creamery, is a real standout. While their delicious ice cream, frozen yogurt, and sherbet are all made on-site, it's possible that the very best thing about this creamery is its handmade waffle cone, the smell of which will begin to entice you before you even reach your ice cream destination. The warm aroma of baking waffle cones has lured me (and countless other ice cream fans) to Acushnet Creamery for years.

ice cream with spanish olive oil

SERVES 4

I first heard about this combination from my friend Brian Knowles, who tasted this dish at a party hosted by his friend Heather Atwood, a Gloucester-based food writer. I was instantly intrigued. Brian raved about it so much that I had to try it. This simple combination pairs surprisingly well together. Make sure you use only the best quality ice cream and olive oil—it will make all the difference. This dish is great on its own or served with the almond citrus biscotti.

1   quart premium vanilla ice cream
1/4 cup (or to taste) excellent quality Spanish olive oil

1. Divide vanilla ice cream among serving dishes. Place in freezer until ready to serve.
2. When ready to serve, remove dishes from freezer and drizzle each with 1 tablespoon of olive oil. Serve immediately.

almond citrus biscotti

MAKES APPROXIMATELY 12 SLICES

Hints of orange and honey lace these crunchy biscotti, which are great as a light dessert or snack with a cup of coffee or tea.

1   cup plus 2 tablespoons flour, plus extra for dusting
1/4 cup plus 1 tablespoon cornmeal
1/4 cup sugar
1   teaspoon baking powder
    Pinch of kosher salt
2   large eggs
1   tablespoon honey
    Zest of 1 large orange
    Juice of 1/2 large orange
1   teaspoon vanilla extract
1/2 cup marcona almonds, roughly chopped

1. Preheat oven to 350°F.
2. Line a baking sheet with parchment paper and set aside.
3. In a medium bowl, whisk flour, cornmeal, sugar, baking powder, and salt and set aside.
4. In a small bowl, combine eggs, honey, orange zest and juice, and vanilla. Add to dry ingredients and mix until well combined. Add almonds. Using your hands, continue to mix until dough is completely combined (add more flour to dough if it's sticky).
5. Dust hands with flour and form dough into a log about 9 inches long by 4 inches wide. Gently flatten. Transfer dough to baking sheet and bake until lightly golden in color, about 15-20 minutes. Remove from oven and let cool for 10 minutes.
6. Using a serrated knife, carefully cut log into 1/2-inch thick slices. Lay slices cut-side down on same baking sheet and bake for another 10 minutes. Turn slices and bake until golden brown, about 5-10 minutes.
7. Cool completely on wire rack. Store in airtight container for up to 1 week.

cook's note: Marcona almonds are native to Spain and are slightly smaller, rounder, and sweeter than regular almonds. They are usually available at gourmet food shops. If you can't find them, substitute with whole, unsalted almonds.

afternoon applesauce cake with spiced whipped cream

SERVES 8-10

This cake has all the homey flavors of a New England autumn. It is great warm or at room temperature, served with a dollop of this delicious spiced whipped cream. Like most baked goods, this cake is best served the day it's made, but will keep up to 2 days. If you don't have a springform pan, use any 9-inch baking pan—just be sure to line the bottom with parchment paper and give it a good coat of cooking spray. You can also make this cake in a square pan, which makes it more kid-friendly.

Cooking spray
2   cups flour
1   tablespoon baking powder
2   teaspoons cinnamon
1/2 teaspoon ground nutmeg
1/2 teaspoon baking soda
1/2 teaspoon kosher salt
1/4 teaspoon ground cloves
1   stick unsalted butter, at room temperature
1   cup packed light brown sugar
2   large eggs
1   teaspoon vanilla extract
1   cup unsweetened applesauce

Spiced Whipped Cream
1   cup heavy whipping cream
2   tablespoons sugar
1/2 teaspoon vanilla extract
1/4 teaspoon cinnamon
1/8 teaspoon ground nutmeg

1. Preheat oven to 350°F.
2. Place a 9-inch round springform pan on a baking sheet. Coat pan on bottom and sides with cooking spray and set aside.
3. In a medium bowl, combine flour, baking powder, cinnamon, nutmeg, baking soda, salt, and cloves and set aside.
4. Using an electric mixer, beat butter and brown sugar until combined. Add eggs one at a time, beating after each addition. Add vanilla, increase speed to medium-high, and beat until light and fluffy, about 2 minutes. Add applesauce and mix, scraping down sides of bowl to incorporate everything together (mixture will look separated because of applesauce; it will blend together once you add flour mixture). Slowly add in flour mixture and mix until just combined.
5. Pour batter evenly in prepared pan and rap against counter once or twice to release any air bubbles. Bake until golden brown and a toothpick inserted into center comes out clean, about 35-40 minutes.
6. Remove from oven and cool in pan for about 15 minutes. Run a knife around edge of cake to loosen, remove from pan, and serve warm, or allow to cool completely on a wire rack.
7. Make whipped cream. Using an electric mixer, whip cream, sugar, cinnamon, nutmeg, ginger, and cloves until medium peaks form.
8. Serve cake with a dollop of whipped cream.

COFFEE MILK

I had never heard of coffee milk until I moved to the South Coast—and chances are, if you're not from around here, you might not have either—but one sip of this creamy concoction was all it took for me to get hooked.

Coffee milk is similar to chocolate milk except that the milk is flavored with coffee syrup. Coffee syrup has been around for decades, dating back to the 1930s when the Eclipse brand of coffee syrup was first introduced. The Autocrat brand soon followed, creating a rivalry among the two for decades. (The feud is no longer, as Autocrat now owns both brands.) Other brands later emerged to keep up with the demand for this curious local product.

Coffee milk is so popular in Rhode Island (and in other pockets of Southern New England) that residents declared it the state's official drink in 1993. (Coffee milk even beat out Del's Lemonade.) The drink now has a solid presence in diners, restaurants, and even on some college campuses across the area. Despite its local popularity, the drink is all but impossible to find outside of the region (but don't despair, you can order coffee syrup online).

Making coffee milk is as easy as it gets: combine milk and coffee syrup. But the coffee syrup you use will definitely impact the flavor. In the name of research, I've tried them all. Autocrat and Eclipse are the sweetest varieties on the market. Eclipse boasts a slightly rounder, softer flavor with hints of vanilla. For me (and all of my faithful testers), there was one clear winner: Dave's Coffee from Charlestown, RI. For a real coffee flavor, it won hands down.

Dave's Coffee starts with roasted Brazilian beans, which they rest for two days. The beans are then cold-brewed into coffee for eighteen hours before mixing with cane sugar. The blend is simmered down into a rich syrup that is full of tantalizing coffee flavor.

Dave's Coffee is a certified organic coffee roaster and a member of Farm Fresh Rhode Island, which unites local Rhode Island food producers with consumers, restaurants, and markets. This family-owned business is dedicated to providing a great product made by people in the community. Dave's Coffee syrup is worth searching out at gourmet food shops, Whole Food Markets across the region, or online, because, in the end, taste matters.

creamy coffee milk pudding

SERVES 6

When I moved to the South Coast, I fell in love with coffee milk at first sip. Here, the drink is transformed into a creamy, decadent dessert with just the right amount of coffee flavor, worthy of any special occasion.

¼ cup sugar
2 tablespoons cornstarch
¼ teaspoon kosher salt
1 cup milk
1 cup heavy cream
½ cup coffee syrup (see cook's note)
1 teaspoon vanilla extract
6 ounces white chocolate chips
1 tablespoon unsalted butter
   Fresh whipped cream, for garnish, optional
   Finely grated coffee beans, for garnish, optional

1. Gather 6 short serving dishes (or glasses) and set aside.
2. Whisk together sugar, cornstarch, and salt in a medium saucepan.
3. In a medium bowl, combine milk, heavy cream, coffee syrup, and vanilla. Whisk into dry mixture until combined.
4. Place saucepan over medium-high heat. Cook, whisking continuously, until mixture has thickened, about 15 minutes. If mixture starts to boil, lower heat to medium while it cooks.
5. When thickened, add white chocolate and whisk until completely melted. Remove from heat and stir in butter until melted.
6. Ladle pudding into serving dishes (or glasses) and cover tightly with plastic wrap, placing it directly on surface of pudding to prevent a skin from forming.
7. Refrigerate until set, at least 2 hours. Serve cold with whipped cream and a dusting of coffee beans (if using).

cook's note: Not all coffee syrups are created equal. I recommend using Dave's Coffee from Rhode Island. It has a pure coffee flavor that isn't too sweet and provides just the right balance. (With other brands you will have to adjust the sugar in the recipe, because they tend to be much sweeter and have less coffee flavor.)

cranberry applesauce

MAKES APPROXIMATELY 4 CUPS

Bright red cranberries look like little jewels among
diced apples as they simmer together in a pot
on the stove. Slowly they begin to tint the apples,
making for a subtle red hue that not only adds an
unexpected color but also a slightly tart flavor to
this traditional applesauce recipe. This sauce is a
perfect way to usher in fall; it also makes a great
side dish for holiday entertaining.

8   medium Macintosh apples, peeled, cored,
    and diced
2   cups fresh or frozen cranberries
4   cups water
    Juice of 2 lemons
1/2 cup sugar, or to taste

1. Combine apples and cranberries in a large Dutch
   oven. Add water, lemon juice, and sugar and stir to
   coat everything. Bring to a boil; reduce heat to
   simmer until apples and cranberries are tender,
   stirring occasionally, about 30 minutes (you should
   be able to easily pop cranberries with back of a
   wooden spoon when done).
2. Remove from heat. For chunkier applesauce, mash
   with a potato masher. For a smoother consistency,
   purée in a food processor. Taste for flavor and add
   more sugar if applesauce is too tart.
3. Transfer to a bowl and refrigerate until ready to
   serve. Serve cold or at room temperature.

   cook's note: This homemade applesauce will
   keep refrigerated in an airtight container for up
   to 2 weeks.

sunset ice cream cake

SERVES 8

As the name implies, this cake is inspired by the colors of the sunset. (Ned's Point in Mattapoisett is one of my favorite sunset spots.) It's a great dessert for a summer party, especially since it needs to be made in advance—no last minute assembly required! Feel free to use this version as inspiration, and design your own cake with you own color or flavor combinations. One thing to keep in mind is that ice cream flavors with multiple ingredients (such as cookies 'n cream or mint chocolate chip) can look a little messy in the cake. If you're looking for a stunning visual effect, single flavored ice creams and sorbets, like the ones used here, make for the cleanest, most striking presentation.

1 pint vanilla ice cream
1 pint mango sorbet
1 pint raspberry sorbet

1. Line bottom and sides of a loaf pan with plastic wrap, making sure there is enough overhang on long sides to be able to lift out frozen cake later. Place pan in freezer for about 1 hour.
2. Remove vanilla ice cream from freezer and allow to soften.
3. When loaf pan is cold, scoop softened vanilla ice cream into bottom of pan and spread evenly with a spatula. Gently press ice cream down in pan, creating a nice, even layer of ice cream. Cover top of ice cream loosely with plastic wrap and place back in freezer for 30 minutes.
4. Remove mango sorbet from freezer and allow to soften.
5. Remove pan from freezer and remove plastic wrap from top. Spread softened mango sorbet evenly over vanilla ice cream layer, using a spatula or back of a spoon. Cover top of sorbet loosely with plastic wrap and place back in freezer for 30 minutes.
6. Remove raspberry sorbet from freezer and allow to soften.
7. Remove pan from freezer and remove plastic wrap from top. Spread softened raspberry sorbet evenly over mango sorbet layer, using a spatula or back of a spoon. Cover top of sorbet loosely with plastic wrap and place back in freezer for 30 minutes.
8. To unmold cake from pan, carefully run a sharp paring knife along outside edge, between layer of plastic and pan (taking care not to pierce cake). Slightly tug on plastic, gauging if ice cream cake will easily release. If it doesn't, run knife along edge again. Pull any plastic wrap away from top of ice cream cake and place a rectangular platter over top of cake so that when you invert it, cake will fit nicely over plate (you don't want any plastic getting stuck under cake once it's inverted). Invert pan so that cake unmolds onto serving platter. Smooth out any uneven edges with a warm knife. Cover cake loosely with plastic wrap and freeze until ready to serve.

cook's note: When layering, try to work as quickly as you can to prevent layer(s) of ice cream and sorbet from melting and blending together.

general index

ingredient index

APPLES
Afternoon applesauce cake with spiced whipped
  cream, 209
Brussels sprouts salad with apples, 63
Cranberry applesauce, 212
Old-fashioned pancakes with apple butter, 20
Russian kale + apple salad, 53

AVOCADO
Beer-battered fish tacos with creamy lime guacamole, 152
East Coast Cobb salad, 148
Lemony quinoa salad with avocado + sprouts, 83

BEERS, WINES, CHAMPAGNES + SPIRITS
Beach plum mojito, 99
Chicken Madeira with creamy mashed potatoes, 192
Chilled saketini, 98
Grilled hot dogs with spicy beer mustard, 140
Mussels with white wine, butter, herbs + sourdough, 165
Red wine truffles, 202
Spicy Bloody Mary, 9
Steamed clams in garlic, lemon + beer broth, 38
Sunday morning mimosa, 9
White wine sangria, 98

BLUEBERRIES, STRAWBERRIES + CRANBERRIES
Blueberry lemonade, 79
Cranberry applesauce, 212
Fresh cranberry smoothie, 79
Fresh-picked blueberry muffins, 17
Jalapeño + cheddar cornbread with cranberry butter, 190
Petite blueberry hand pies, 92
Pick-your-own strawberry milkshakes, 202
Strawberry salsa with sugared pita chips, 88
Vanilla panna cotta with berries, shortbread crumble
  + lemon granita, 204

BREADS, BISCUITS + PASTRIES
Almond citrus biscotti, 207
Black pepper biscuits, 25
Bread + garlic soup with rhubarb compote + garden
  blossoms, 36
Cloumage pizza with garden greens, 55
Crostini: ricotta + local honey; fresh mozzarella + roasted
  garlicky tomatoes; fresh pea purée, prosciutto
  + Parmesan, 109
Crostini with wilted kale + goat cheese, 111
Grilled heirloom tomato + mozzarella pizza, 134
Homemade pizza dough, 135
Jalapeño + cheddar cornbread with cranberry butter, 190
Roasted garlic bread with fresh herbs, 185

Rustic Mediterranean panzanella, 63
Sweet bread French toast with honey butter, 22
Whole wheat pumpkin scones, 23

BRUSSELS SPROUTS + CAULIFLOWER
Brussels sprouts salad with apples, 63
Roasted cauliflower with Parmesan, 182

CAKES
Afternoon applesauce cake with spiced whipped
  cream, 209
Cinnamon crumb coffee cake, 16
Old-fashioned pancakes with apple butter, 20

CHEESES
Baked Brie with honey + almonds, 107
Burgers with aged cheddar + homemade tomato jam, 136
Cloumage pizza with garden greens, 55
Crostini: ricotta + local honey; fresh mozzarella + roasted
  garlicky tomatoes; fresh pea purée, prosciutto
  + Parmesan, 109
Crostini with wilted kale + goat cheese, 111
Deep-dish quiche with onion, spinach + salty feta, 13
Grilled radicchio with Great Hill Blue + walnuts, 140
Grilled heirloom tomato + mozzarella pizza, 134
Heirloom tomatoes with feta + olives, 72
Homemade ricotta gnocchi, 194
Jalapeño + cheddar cornbread with cranberry butter, 190
Macaroni with heirloom tomato sauce + fresh chevre, 186
Roasted beet salad with goat cheese + pistachios, 51
Serrano + Manchego sandwich with quince, 42
Zucchini ribbons with creamy goat cheese dressing, 71

CHOCOLATE
Campfire brownies, 90
Creamy coffee milk pudding, 211
Red wine truffles, 202

CITRUS
Almond citrus biscotti, 207
Blueberry lemonade, 79
Grilled corn with jalapeño-lime butter, 143
Lemony kale hummus, 80
Lemony quinoa salad with avocado + sprouts, 83
Raw corn salad with lime vinaigrette, 61
Roasted salmon + potato salad with lemon-caper pesto, 160
Sunday morning mimosa, 9

MEAT
Applewood smoked bacon + onion crostata, 193
Bacon jam, 24
Burgers with aged cheddar + homemade tomato jam, 136
Chouriço in puff pastry, 105
Chouriço-stuffed mushrooms, 114
Chouriço-stuffed pork loin with garlic mash, 180–181
Crispy polenta with sausage ragu, 183
Grilled flank steak with fresh rosemary, 127
Grilled hot dogs with spicy beer mustard, 140
Grilled leg of lamb with greens + lemon yogurt, 128
Macomber turnip hash with shredded pork + eggs, 196
Portuguese kale soup, 32
Serrano + Manchego sandwich with quince, 42
Tomato toasts with Serrano ham, 127
Yankee pot roast, 170

NUTS
Almond citrus biscotti, 207
Baked Brie with honey + almonds, 107
Grilled radicchio with Great Hill Blue + walnuts, 140
Roasted beet salad with goat cheese + pistachios, 51

ONION, GARLIC + CHIVE
Applewood smoked bacon + onion crostata, 193
Bread + garlic soup with rhubarb compote + garden
    blossoms, 36
Chouriço-stuffed pork loin with garlic mash, 180
Egg salad tartine with breakfast radishes + chives, 41
Fresh mozzarella + roasted garlicky tomatoes, 109
Garlic chive scrambled eggs, 19
Green salad with fresh herb vinaigrette + chive
    blossoms, 67
Grilled shrimp with garlic, 150
Roasted garlic bread with fresh herbs, 185
Steamed clams in garlic, lemon + beer broth, 38

PASTA
Chiocciole pasta salad with yogurt dressing, 83
Homemade ricotta gnocchi, 194
Macaroni with heirloom tomato sauce + fresh chevre, 186
Spring pasta with asparagus + poached egg, 54
Sweet potato ravioli salad with greens + walnut oil, 176–177

POTATOES
Chicken Madeira with creamy mashed potatoes, 192
Chouriço-stuffed pork loin with garlic mash, 180
Grilled swordfish + potatoes with thyme-infused
    mayonnaise, 154
Roasted salmon + potato salad with lemon-caper pesto, 160
Smashed potato salad, 73
Sweet potato ravioli salad with greens + walnut oil, 176–177

POULTRY
Backyard BBQ chicken, 130
Chicken Madeira with creamy mashed potatoes, 192
Crispy chicken with parsley pesto, 188
Grilled chicken with fresh oregano vinaigrette, 132
Pan-roasted duck with toasted farro, kale + rainier cherry
    mostarda, 178
Turkey burgers with smoky chipotle ketchup, 131

ROOT VEGETABLES
Egg salad tartine with breakfast radishes + chives, 41
Garden carrot soup, 41
Lemon cucumber + radish salad, 53
Macomber turnip hash with shredded pork + eggs, 196
Roasted beet salad with goat cheese + pistachios, 51

SHELLFISH
Baked scallops with toasted breadcrumbs, 150
Chilled paella salad with shrimp, 82
Chilled sweet corn soup with lobster, 35
Classic shrimp bisque, 172
Crab cakes with Old Bay aioli, 104
East Coast Cobb salad, 148
Grilled oysters: mignonette; spicy sriracha butter;
    casino style, 124–125
Grilled shrimp with garlic, 150
Modern clams casino with oregano mojo, 117
Mussels with white wine, butter, herbs + sourdough, 165
New England cioppino with toasted baguette, 30
Seared scallops with corn risotto + basil oil, 153
Shrimp tacos with cucumber salsa, 159
Shrimp toasts with scallions, ginger + sesame, 115
Steamed clams in garlic, lemon + beer broth, 38
Watch Hill oyster chowder, 31

SQUASH + ZUCCHINI
Free-form garden lasagna, 70
Roasted butternut squash soup with maple cream, 38
Roasted zucchini + summer squash salad with creamy basil
    vinaigrette, 68
Zucchini ribbons with creamy goat cheese dressing, 71

TOMATOES
Burgers with aged cheddar + homemade tomato jam, 136
Crispy polenta with sausage ragu, 183
End-of-the-season tomato risotto, 174
Free-form garden lasagna, 70
Fresh mozzarella + roasted garlicky tomatoes, 109
Grilled heirloom tomato + mozzarella pizza, 134
Heirloom tomatoes with feta + olives, 72
Macaroni with heirloom tomato sauce + fresh chevre, 186
Rustic Mediterranean panzanella, 63
Simple year-round tomato sauce, 72
Spicy Bloody Mary, 9
Tomato toasts with Serrano ham, 127
Yellow tomato gazpacho, 80